Wiring
Guide 2020

The Complete Indoor And Outdoor Wiring Guide Including Smart Home Wiring In 2020

Neal Johnson

Table of Contents

Introduction

The installation of a new wiring system or the upgrade of an existing one is not an uphill task. But it is a process-laden experience that requires knowledge of the recommended testing and installation procedures. Moreover, emerging technologies, such as the Internet of Things (IoT), have broadened the scope and functionality of wiring and other electrical processes.

This book is designed to help you learn and perform a wide range of wiring tasks and spare yourself the effort and cost of hiring technicians. It is a step-by-step guide for a broad range of wiring procedures. The different chapters will equip you with the skills for performing electrical tasks, such as indoor and outdoor wiring, as well as Wi-Fi and smart home installations.

Chapter One: Wiring Operations

The electrical power ecosystem consists of a variety of network components and installations that support the generation, distribution, and consumption of electrical energy. This ecosystem relies on the wiring system to power the functional and operational elements within it.

A wiring system allows you to supply electrical current to the different components and fixtures in your home. You need a wiring system to connect lights, receptacles, switches, lamps, and fans, as well as other accessories and home appliances. A robust wiring system consists of a network of wires and cables that transmit power between the main distribution board and the designated destination points. The flow of power in your wiring system begins from the meter board of your supplier to the various indoor and outdoor locations.

Electrical wiring operations are based on structured methods. Your home wiring tasks involve either the joint box or looping system, depending on your preferred wiring plans and design.

The joint box system is a wiring method that involves attaching different wires together to establish the connections required to support the flow of electric current to fixtures and outlets. Install relevant connectors to create joints within the joint boxes. As such, this method does not involve a lot of cabling because the joints within the joint boxes will perform much of the power distribution functions. However, the simple structure of the joint system is not sufficient to sustain long term electric wiring installations. This method is ideal for temporary use in your outbuildings or outdoor structures.

The looping system is the most ideal choice for installing a wiring system in your home. Also known as a loop-in system, this particular method is considered to be the universally recommended approach to electrical wiring. The looping system distributes energy in a parallel format that allows you to provide individual controls for every single outlet or fixture.

The loop-in dynamics of the method are responsible for bringing a feed conductor into contact with a terminal to create a connection to a fixture or outlet. The loop-in mechanism then conveys the feed conductor to the next point requiring a connection, effectively creating a pattern of loops linked to different points requiring power supply. For example, if you want to create a connection for your light bulb, the loop-in system will automatically set the feed conductor in motion and it toward the terminal. The same procedure applies when creating a connection for a switch, socket, fan, or any other fixture in your wiring network. However, there are requirements that must be met when setting the transmission of loops in the cables. For example, looping the live wire from a fixture, such as a light, is forbidden. Rather, you should loop the live wire conductor in the meter board. Looping of a neutral wire is a bit flexible, as you can do it from either the meter board or any fixture.

Deployment of the looping method in your home wiring presents you with various advantages. This includes cost savings because this method is not dependent on joint boxes. This method also spares you the task of hiding joints in different parts of the building, including the floor and the ceiling. However, there are also several downsides associated with this method. You need a lot of cables and wires to implement the looping method.

Preliminary Preparations
There are several preliminary preparations that you must perform before you get down to work. One of the major mistakes that you can commit is to begin an electrical wiring project before securing the relevant approval from the building department. Visit your local

building department and seek the relevant approval required to implement your home wiring project. This includes a permit and appointment schedules for the rough-in inspection during wiring and a final inspection after completion.

When you apply for the relevant permits, take with you the sketch of the wiring system you want to implement indoors, outdoors, or both. The sketch should basically show the scope of your wiring and the positions of the key components, including lighting and outlet locations. It will form the basis for the site inspection at the rough-in and completion stages of your wiring. The inspector will either approve or decline your approval request depending on whether or not your wiring plan meets the required thresholds. Be prepared to answer any questions or address the concerns that the inspector might have about your wiring system. Be ready to accommodate any revisions that the inspector might suggest before approving your sketches. Failure to observe the approval procedures will land you in trouble with the authorities.

Evaluation of Overall Wiring System

Safety always comes first when determining the design and installation aspects of wiring. There are certain standards that must be observed. The choice of the types of wires or cables, as well as their sizes, is dictated by the strength of the electric current and the levels of the voltage that will be imposed on the electrical circuits. As such, the design and components of your entire wiring system must adhere to the recommended threshold for electric current and voltage. This includes the scope of protection and control measures within the circuit and the devices associated with the distribution of electric current within the wiring system.

The design and complexity of your indoor or outdoor wiring will depend on the nature and location of the project. The installation of wiring in a new house will be a lesser task compared to upgrading an existing wiring system. An old wiring system requires more effort to figure out the cabling paths and faulty installations.

However, the evaluation of your electrical wiring system relative to other utility systems in the house is a very important step to begin with. You may want to understand how your wiring plan relates to your plumbing system, regardless of whether the house is new or not. Knowing the position of the plumbing, both indoors and outdoors, will help you determine the appropriate location for laying your wiring system.

The initial step for old system evaluation is to shut off the power at the main circuit breaker of the service panel. Shut down all the sub-panel and branch circuits, as well, just in case some components of the main breaker panel have malfunctioned due to the passage of time. A non-contact voltage tester will be useful to probe the power flow in the service panel before you embark on your wiring upgrade mission.

Locate and inspect all the crucial components of the existing wiring ecosystem, including circuit breakers, junction boxes, electrical boxes, outlets, receptacles, cabling, and the conduit. You are likely to discover faulty installation, like damaged cables, exposed splices, and blown up fuses, among others. This will involve a lot of work that will include the removal of the drywall and box covers to access the concealed installations. For outdoor installations, this may involve a bit of digging out the soil to ascertain the exact location of the buried conduit or cables. Some physical damages will be visible, while others may need a bit of probing and scanning using the relevant tools.

All plans that concern the connection of your new house to an electricity network must be done in collaboration with your power service provider. The distance of the service provider's power pole and the type of the main service line connection phase are some of the key areas to focus on when evaluating the installation of a wiring system in a new house. The utility provider's power pole should be close enough for the convenience of connecting to your house. You will also want to know if the main power line is a three-phase or a single phase. This is easy to tell because a single-phase connection will have two electric wire conductors running between the power provider's pole next to your house and the pole of the main power distribution line. This means a single-phase connection has only one hot wire and one neutral wire. A three-phase connection has four conductors representing two hot wires, a neutral wire, and a grounding wire. Such variations should inform your overall wiring plan because a three-phase connection carries higher voltage or electric current compared to a single-phase connection.

The drainage system, plumbing network, and underground cables crossing through your home to other parts of your neighborhood are worth probing during the evaluation stage of your outdoor wiring. It will be risky to dig trenches for your wiring network without the knowledge of the exact location of the underground infrastructure for the other utilities. You will require the help of your local building inspection office to perform this kind of evaluation. In fact, some local authorities require that you obtain a license before digging trenches for electrical wiring or plumbing in your compound.

The entire evaluation process should give you a clearer picture of the requirements for the kind of indoor or outdoor wiring plan you want to install. In some cases, it makes sense to pull out the entire wiring system in an old house and install a new one, especially if the old system has been rendered irrelevant by changes and updates to the National Electrical Code (NEC) requirements.

Wiring Plan and Design

Electrical diagrams are crucial in the planning and preparation phase of your wiring operations. Wiring diagrams are particularly helpful in mapping out the overall profile of the building and its electrical installations. The visual representation of risk factors allows you to identify and avoid potential accidents or injuries during the actual installation of the wiring system. It is also important to generate a visual representation of the actual physical positioning and interconnection of components, such as junction boxes, panels, and sub-panels, among others.

A wiring diagram is best outlined in a schematic format that captures the visual aspects of the physical connections and their relationship to the overall design of the electrical system. A schematic wiring diagram shows the network of all your electrical connections, including the actual positioning of fixtures and components. The representation of the physical arrangement of components allows you to determine the layout and interconnection of electrical wires within the system. The image below demonstrates the basic representation of a schematic wiring diagram.

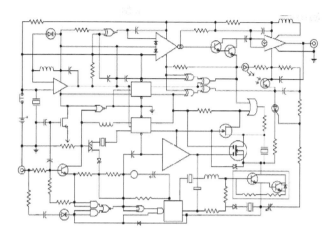

The representation of your wiring diagram will ideally be unique to your house design and your preferences for the electrical installations. However, there are general guidelines that you need to follow when preparing your diagram. For example, it is wise to begin determining the relevant electrical symbols before proceeding to draw line diagrams depicting the circuit or layout. This ordinarily leads you to the next phase of positioning your chosen symbols and establishing connections between them within the circuit. Remember to deploy lie hops in areas where electrical wires will be crossing over each other. Finally, apply layers to demonstrate levels of sophistication or the complexity of the wiring diagram.

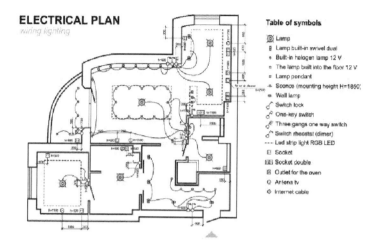

ELECTRICAL PLAN
wiring lighting

Table of symbols

- Lamp
- Lamp built-in swivel dual
- Built-in halogen lamp 12 V
- The lamp built into the floor 12 V
- Lamp pendant
- Sconce (mounting height H=1850')
- Wall lamp
- Switch lock
- One-key switch
- Three gangs one way switch
- Switch rheostat (dimer)
- Led strip light RGB LED
- Socket
- Socket double
- Outlet for the oven
- Antena tv
- Internet cable

National Electrical Code

The National Electrical Code (NEC) is the reference point for all requirements that concern the installation of electrical systems. All the safety precautions and structural thresholds that you must observe when performing electrical tasks, or when implementing electrical projects, are contained in this code. Make sure you familiarize yourself with the NEC requirements before carrying out your first DIY electrical wiring project in your home.

The ground-fault circuit interrupter (GFCI) and the arc-fault circuit interrupter (AFCI) are some of the common NEC requirements that you will come across in relation to the regulatory requirements for kitchen and bedroom circuit installations. These requirements are discussed in greater detail in chapter two of this book, under the "Receptacles" subtopic.

Overall Wiring Code Requirements

NEC requirements are meant to guide you on the unique aspects of every room and each of the appliances in your house. The code covers broad areas and may vary from state to state. This chapter highlights requirements that concern kitchen, bathroom, laundry, and outdoor wiring. The focus on these particular areas is informed by the unique nature of their wiring installations. We will also be looking at the relevant codes for lighting fixtures and their significance to your overall wiring system.

The common code requirements relating to the entire house give prominence to outlet wiring and circuits. Outlet circuits for lighting fixtures must be sufficiently distributed throughout the house with a recommended maximum floor space of 575 square feet, according to the NEC requirements.

Installation of AFCI protection in bedroom outlets is a compulsory requirement. All bathroom receptacle installations must bear GFCI protection, as well. You must also have a dedicated circuit of no less than 20 amps for each bathroom. The other key requirements for the bathroom include the wall installation of receptacles at maximum distances of 3 feet from basins. You are also required to avoid positioning receptacles directly over your bathtub. GFCI protection is similarly a compulsory requirement for any outlet that is installed within close proximity to a sink in the bathroom or a garage.

Your laundry room is similarly subject to the NEC-stipulated thresholds. The receptacles in your laundry room should have no less than 20-amp circuits. Moreover, the circuit for the laundry receptacle should not be connected to any other outlets. The same requirement applies to the circuit for your dryer. The dryer actually requires circuits with a minimum of 30 amps.

Your basement must have a GFCI-protected outlet, even if it is still under construction. However, there are GFCI installation exceptions for outlets in certain areas that are ordinarily inaccessible, such as the ones in the ceiling of your garage.

It is compulsory to install receptacles in any wall that measures more than 2 feet wide. To this end, this requirement applies to any other wall-like structure, such as counter partitions. There is also a 6-feet minimum threshold for the interval distance between receptacles along the horizontal plane of a wall. You must also install receptacles in hallways with lengths of over 10 feet. It is also important to bear in mind that the maximum NEC-recommended height for receptacles is 5.5 inches. But the doorways and the fireplace in your house do count toward these requirements for wall receptacles because they ordinarily cannot accommodate electrical installations.

When it comes to light switches, there are certain provisions of the NEC that must be observed for your wiring to be considered compliant. For example, you are required to install a lighting outlet that is controlled by a wall switch in every single room in your house. Moreover, with the exception of the bathroom and kitchen, you have the liberty to install switched receptacles in the lighting outlets for all the other rooms in your house, according to the NEC requirements.

There are also requirements for installing lighting in other parts of the house. including the staircase, the hallway, and the garage. Each of these areas must be supplied accordingly, with lighting outlets and their respective wall switches. You will also need to install switches at every entrance if the staircase in your house stretches for more than six levels. With the exception of garage vehicle doors, you will need to install lighting outlets in main entrances, including the exterior side of your front and back doors, as well as the egress doors for the garage, according to the NEC requirements.

Circuiting Fundamentals

Determine the nature and scope of your electrical circuit well in advance to align it with the overall wiring system. You may choose to go with either the series or parallel circuit.

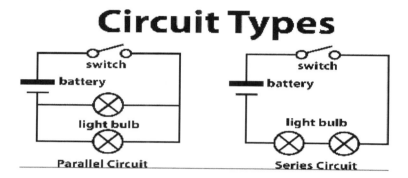

Circuit Types

The series type provides a single electricity transmission path because the linear arrangement of the resistors restricts the flow of electric current to the single path. Clearly, this is not an ideal choice because of the limitations associated with the restrictions on the flow of the electric current. It will particularly pose a problem if different fixtures share a single path of current flow. The voltage allocation for each load or fixture will dip with the increase of the number of fixtures because each resistor in the chain carries the same amount of electric current. This results in a situation where the combined voltage of all the resistors in the chain is equivalent to that of a single resistor. For example, if you plug an iron box in a socket that is installed on a series circuit, your lightbulbs will dim because of current reduction. When a single fixture malfunctions, the entire circuit is rendered redundant. If a bulb blows, the other bulbs won't light until you replace the malfunctioned one to complete the circuit.

A parallel circuit, on the other hand, is considered to be best suited for use in homes because it supports the flow of electricity on multiple paths. Each of the loads operates independently, such that the addition or removal of any fixture or appliance will leave the flow of electricity uninterrupted. The interruption of the pathway will in no way affect the flow of electricity. If one bulb blows, the rest of the bulbs and outlets will continue to function because of their circuit independence. This offers the flexibility of operating multiple loads without compromising the flow of electric current to each of the loads. The different fixtures and appliances draw energy from a shared source of electric power that transmits constant voltage. This is the kind of circuit you will need to implement if you want an efficient wiring system for the household receptacles in your home

The failure to follow proper circuitry procedures will expose you to inconsistent power supply issues due to incidences of short-circuiting. A short circuit is triggered by the flow of electric current beyond the boundaries of a particular circuit. This occurs when loose or exposed live wires within the wiring system or in appliances rub against each other. That is the reason why old wiring systems with bare or damaged wires are prone to short circuits. This is one area you should focus on when upgrading an existing wiring system in your home. Moreover, do not leave behind loose hanging wires in your circuit to avoid short-circuiting complications in your wiring system.

Kitchen Circuitry and Wiring Requirements

You are required to accord the kitchen some special attention during wiring implementation because of the high voltage of electric current required to power appliances. The nature and scope of circuits in the kitchen are determined by the type of each appliance. The lighting, dishwasher, electric range, garbage disposal, microwave, refrigerator, and all other small appliances you intend to have in your kitchen should inform your wiring decisions.

There are recommended specifications for installing the GFCI and AFCI in the kitchen. For example, there is a 48-inch maximum spacing interval imposed on GFCI installations for countertops. In other words, you need to fix your receptacles in frequent intervals to provide convenience for plugging in your countertop appliances.

You will end up overstretching the cables or cords of your appliances if you choose to space your countertop GFCI installations far apart from each other.

The minimum recommended amperage and voltage of the circuit for kitchen lighting is 15 amps and 120 volts, respectively. This requirement spreads across all lighting fixtures, including ceiling lights and cabinet lights, as well as recessed lights. Kitchen lighting fixtures and installations do not require GFCI connection because they do not operate on high amperage. In fact, a GFCI connection will expose your kitchen lighting to the potential of tripping alongside the other receptacle installations in the event of an electrical fault.

The other key safety requirement for kitchen wiring installations is the use of tamper-proof outlets. Every single outlet for the different receptacles in the kitchen must bear designs that resist tampering by foreign objects. This requirement was introduced with children in mind because of the potentially devastating risks of inserting objects in the outlets. This will be a requirement of major concern if you are upgrading the wiring system of an old house. You should replace all the non-complying receptacle outlets that were installed before this requirement took effect.

A dishwasher requires a dedicated circuit because it consumes more electricity than other ordinary kitchen appliances. It is recommended that you use a circuit of at least 15 amps and an electric current averaging 120 and 125 volts. The size specification for wire is 14 gauge with a ground. Just like the kitchen lighting, you do not have to connect the dishwasher to the GFCI. A dedicated circuit is sufficient to supply the power needs of this particular appliance. That is because the short cable run of the dishwasher makes it susceptible to high initial electric current flow when turned on. A dedicated circuit is meant to protect other electrical installations in the kitchen from the frequent tripping of power that may be occasioned by sudden surges of electrical current whenever the dishwasher is turned on.

An electric range requires a dedicated and powerful circuit, preferably 50 amps, and a high-voltage. You need a current of 240 and 250 volts to power an electric range efficiently. The recommended electrical wire size specification is 6-gauge non-metallic cable. There are alternative high-density wires and cables that you can use in your circuit for the electric range, such as 6 THHN conduit-wrapped wire. It is advisable to have an electric range in your kitchen wiring plan, regardless of whether or not you have one. The electric range outlet may be required in the future when you acquire one or if the ownership of the house changes to people with a preference for this particular circuit installation. The electric range does not require a GFCI connection because its high power consumption will easily trip the circuit breaker.

A garbage disposal operates on the same voltage and wire size requirements as a dishwasher. However, you will need a slightly higher amperage of at least 20 amps for your circuit. Have a dedicated circuit for this circuit installation in your wiring plan for efficiency and convenience purposes. The garbage disposal does not require a GFCI connection because it poses a greater risk of tripping for similar reasons to that of the dishwasher.

The installation of a circuit for a microwave requires 20 amps and an electric current of 120 and 125 volts. It is also recommended that you use a 12-gauge wire size with a ground wire for safety. These specifications show that a microwave can easily share outlets with other small appliances of a similar range. However, large microwaves will require a dedicated circuit for sufficient power supply.

In the past, refrigerators shared circuits with other small appliances in the house. This has since changed because new refrigerator models are best powered by their own dedicated circuits. Do not expect your refrigerator to generate optimum output if you plug it into an ordinary circuit used for small appliances. When building an electric circuit for your refrigerator, you need at least 20 amps and a current averaging 120 and 125 volts. Use the recommended non-metallic wire size of 12 gauge for the circuit.

As for all the other small kitchen appliances, such as blenders and toasters, no less than two 20-amp circuits powered by either 120-volt or 125-volt electric current is required. Basically, the number of circuits should be commensurate with the number of small appliances that are likely to be operated simultaneously. Decide about the number of small appliances you are likely to use and incorporate the details into your wiring plan. You risk experiencing frequent circuit overloads and tripping of your circuit breakers if you install an insufficient number of circuits relative to the number of gadgets that will be in use.

Chapter Summary

- The wiring system is the primary infrastructure for both electric supply and networking in your home.
- National Electrical Code requirements are mandatory for all home wiring projects.
- Kitchen circuitry requires high-voltage wiring components and installations by virtue of the nature of appliances that are used in the kitchen.

In the next chapter, you will learn about the materials and equipment required to implement home wiring projects.

Chapter Two: Materials and Equipment

This chapter provides details about some of the crucial materials and equipment that you will need to successfully implement your home wiring project. Some of the materials are suitable for both indoor and outdoor wiring, while others are exclusive to either. The material and equipment will always vary with the nature and scope of your wiring project. This chapter focuses on the most crucial materials and components you will require to successfully perform your wiring operations.

Calculate the estimate of the materials that you will need for your work to avoid underestimating or overestimating. The actual quantity of materials that you purchase should be slightly more than your estimate to avoid falling short of the materials midway in the project. Costing of these materials is also important to ensure that your project falls within your budgeted expenses.

Gather your tools and equipment to a central place for convenience and ease of reach. Although it may sound obvious, your electrical tools should be always within reach because wiring is laborious operation. For example, you will likely have to keep going up and down a ladder when performing wiring tasks on a ceiling. You will have trouble juggling between locating equipment that is scattered all over the place. A cordless drill, tester, fish tape, screwdriver, hammer, and tape measure are some of the must-have tools for an electrician. The drill should be accompanied by appropriately-sized spade bits required for the job in hand. For example, you will find the ¾-inch spade bit useful for drilling holes in surfaces for your indoor wiring.

You will also need a clipper and stripping tool for cutting and stripping wires, as well as a ladder to scale heights that are beyond reach. The additional tools you may need will vary with the scope of your work. There are complex tasks that may require specialized or more sophisticated tools. For example, you will have to hire a larger drill for areas that require heavy drilling, such as rocky outcrops in your outdoor wiring paths.

It is always important to wear protective gear during your electrical wiring operations. Other than overalls for protection against dirt, consider wearing heavy-duty leather gloves and rubber sole shoes for protection against electric shock from live wires. You might accidentally touch or step on a live wire while going about your wiring chores. Heavy-duty leather gloves are also useful for giving you a firm grip on your tools and instruments.

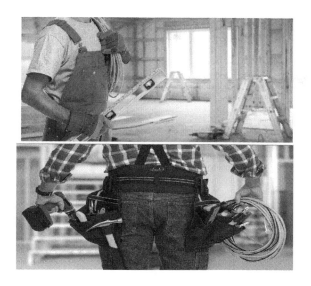

Wires

Wire sizes for house wiring projects vary with the ampacity of the circuits. The American Wire System (AWG) provides the reference points for wire sizes. Gauge is the preferred unit of measurement for wire sizes. Although there are as many gauges as you can imagine, consider selecting the recommended sizes for home wiring, which ranges between 10 and 14 gauge. With safety issues in mind, it is advised to take a conservative approach when choosing your preferred wire size. The ideal approach is to avoid exceeding the maximum watt capacity of your gauge. A range of between 70 to 75 percent of the gauge to watt capacity is sufficient to meet your home wiring needs. For example, a 10-gauge wire is suited for 30 amps. 12-gauge and 14-gauge wire is well suited for 20-amp and 15-amp circuits, respectively. The trend here shows that you need to match lower-sized gauges against circuits with higher amps to supply their high-voltage power needs.

The overlapping relationship between ampacity and wire gauge underscores the diverse nature of their uses. For example, when using non-metallic conductors, NEC regulations prescribe the 14-gauge, 15-amp wire to lighting circuits. 12-gauge, 20-amp wire is ideal for both lighting circuits and refrigeration systems, while 10-gauge, 30-amp is ideal for appliances, such as water heaters and laundry installations, according to the NEC. This shows that the different rooms in your home will feature varying wire sizes with different levels of ampacity, according to the nature of the fixtures and appliances.

Types of Wires

Some of the commonly used wire types in electrical installations include main-feeder, the non-metallic sheathed, the panel feed, the single strand, and the triplex. It is unlikely that you will use main-feeder wire that often because it is mainly used to connect the weather head to the house. But it is important to remember that the cable installation for connecting this type of wire must be able to accommodate 25 percent more of a load than the actual requirements.

You will find a lot of uses for non-metallic sheathed wire, which is alternatively referred to as Rolex wire. This particular type of wire is widely used in home wiring and installations because of its ease of use and suitability for the conditions within a home environment. It has multiple plastic-insulated wires and a bare ground wire, which are held together by a non-metallic wrapping to ensure electrical safety in your house. The Rolex is also cost-friendly compared to other wires of similar use.

Panel feed wire will be equally useful in your house wiring project. Its specifications are well suited for use in powering key components of the wiring network, including the main junction box, and panel installations, like the circuit breaker. Just like with main feeder wire, the cable connecting the panel feed wire must be able to accommodate 25 percent more of a load than the actual requirements.

Single strand wire bears the THHN description and you may find it helpful when you need to use piping to provide protection to individual wires. You can fit multiple single strand wires in it, according to the needs of your overall wiring layout. The single strands are easy to fit in and pull through the piped network of your wiring system.

Triplex wire is mainly used to connect the weather head to the main service line. You will need it if your house is yet to be connected to the power pole. It contains two plastic-coated aluminum wires that are wrapped with a bare ground wire. Triplex wire is designed for use in single-phase power transmission.

Wire Labeling

The NEC has set out a recommended procedure for labeling wires. There are NEC-recommended initials for use as labels on the insulation of wires. These initials include H, HH, N, T, W, and X, and they are meant to guide you on the suitability of wires for different uses and environmental conditions. Initials H and HH denote heat resistance and high heat resistance, respectively. Initial T denotes thermoplastic insulation, with initials W, N, and X denoting wet locations suitability, nylon coated resistant to damage by chemical substances, and flame resistance. These letters are used in different combinations to describe the suitability of wires for different functions. For example, a wire for swimming pool installation will be described by the THW label. Such a wire will be simply referred to as a THW wire. The other widely used labels are THHN wire and XHHN wire, among others.

Cables

Cables should never be confused with wires because, contrary to perception, the two are not the same. Whereas a wire is simply a strand of a conductor material that may be with or without insulation, a cable consists of multiple strands of insulated conductors that are protected under a jacket. Therefore, a thick strand made up of multiple conductors that are not insulated will be classified as a wire because the naked conductor materials touch each other to transmit energy as a single conductor. These differences are important because there are wiring procedures that do not permit the substitution of wires for cables, and vice versa, due to safety concerns.

The number of conductors in a cable is a useful parameter for classifying electrical cables. There are cables that feature a pair of twisted conductors that are insulated within a single jacket. Such cables are classified as twisted-pair cables. A multi-conductor cable classification, on the other hand, consists of more than two insulated conductor materials secured in a single jacket.

Electrical cable sizes should not bother you much because you can always refer to the NEC regulations or make inquiries during purchases. However, it is still important to understand how to determine the appropriate size of cables that you need for your wiring and other electrical needs. Most cables come with the text of specifications stamped on the insulation. Read and note the specifications. Proceed to cut the cable at the edge to have an even surface. This will allow you to get the inches measurement of the cable's cross-section diameter.

The significance of cable size prevails when deciding the cable installation for indoor and outdoor fixtures or receptacles. For example, indoor home lighting will require an electrical cable size of a range of between 1mm and 1.5 mm. 2.5mm cable is still suited for use in domestic wiring operations, as well, but it is best suited for areas with high voltage transmission needs, such as receptacles and circuits. In fact, 2.5mm cable is ideal for transmitting power between circuits and receptacles. Using 2.5mm electrical for your indoor lighting installations will unnecessarily inflate your cost because it is costlier than 1.5mm cable.

It is also important to understand the tension level of your cables, especially when planning outdoor wiring. For example, some cables are described as high tension, while others are classified as low tension. This classification is done on the basis of both the structure and electrical rating of the cables. For example, the structure of a low-tension cable features a higher number of cores than a high-tension cable. This simply means that low-tension cable is heavier and more rigid than high-tension cable. It is for this reason that low-tension cable is used for low voltage power supply, while high-tension cable is used for high-voltage power transmission. It is unlikely that you will find any high-tension electric cable in your home wiring. Low-tension cable is ideal for low-voltage power supply in your outdoor wiring.

Types of Cables

There are different types of cables that are suited for use in either electrical wiring or home networking. Coaxial cable is useful when you need stable signals for installations that convey radio signals. Also known as heliax cable, coaxial cable is particularly handy in the distribution network of your entertainment equipment, such as video and television equipment.

Sheathed cable, be it metallic or non-metallic, is equally useful in your home wiring needs. The metallic sheathed type, or armored cable, consists of three insulated copper wires that are wrapped in a fortified PVC sheathing. It is also known as BX cable and is designed for use in large appliances or for the supply of high-voltage electricity. You may also use metallic sheathed cable with steel sheathing in your outdoor installations.

Non-metallic sheathed cable is the most widely used wiring for homes and residential buildings. It is alternatively referred to as non-metallic building wire and initialized as NM. It contains multiple wires, ranging between and four wires, housed in firm thermoplastic material. The ground wire is bare, while the other wires are coated with plastic insulation. There are upgraded versions of NM cable that are used for outdoor and underground wiring.

Twisted pair cable provides shielded and unshielded options for wiring a building. Shielded twisted pair (STP) cable features two intertwined wires that are insulated. Unshielded twisted pair (UTP) cable, just like STP, features two intertwined wires. However, unlike STP, UTP wires are not insulated to enhance the transmission of signals. This is the cable you should consider using in your indoor multimedia connections because it is cheaper compared to fiber optic and coaxial cable.

The other types of cables that are suitable for home wiring include paired, ribbon, and twin axial cables. Twin-lead cable features double flat wires and they are mostly used to connect antennas to receivers in TVs and other entertainment appliances. Ribbon cable consists of various wire conductors that lie side-by-side on a flat surface in a manner that makes them look like ribbons. It is designed for low-voltage transmission and is widely used in items such as computers and printers. Twinaxial cable is more or less a variation of coaxial cable. The two conductors in twin axial cable is the only feature that makes it different from coaxial cable.

This is not an exhaustive list of the types of cables. This book has focused on the electrical cables that are relevant to home wiring operations. Some of the cables that have been left out are mainly used for large scale operations in industries or electricity generation or transmission. Your choice of any particular cable will depend on the nature of your wiring and the scope of your budget.

Coding of Cable Colors
The standardization of cable colors has not been implemented in the United States, despite being a common practice in many countries around the world. NEC regulations have not imposed any specifications or definitions for color codes. But the coding of the colors is still helpful in determining the live, neutral, and ground conductors. As an electrician, you must be aware that active wires can be anything but yellow, green, yellow-striped green, or light blue.

The Panel

Electrical power flows from the main service line right to your electric meter and the service entrance or main panel. The main panel is more or less a compartment that houses the distribution and control points of electricity power supply. There are also sub-panels that provide extension platforms for managing electrical circuits.

The service panel and the electric meter are more or less twin installations because they are always mounted close to each other. However, it is not mandatory to pair the two. You can mount them separately, as long as they are within close proximity of each other for convenience during wiring operations. You can mount the main panel either indoors or on the outside wall, depending on your preferences to its accessibility. Your choice location must be safe and should be convenient for distributing power to the rest of your house.

Electricity enters the panel through a three-conductor wire that, in turn, distributes power to a network of sub-panels and electrical circuits in different locations within and outside the house. The structure of the main panel is such that it transmits power to the main circuit breaker, which in turn spreads the power to the other sub-panels and electrical circuits. The electric meter plays a crucial role here because it must be connected to complete the circuit and to transmit power to the main circuit breaker through two lugs. There are two live bus bars connected to the circuit breaker and they are responsible for transmitting the electrical power to the other circuit installations. As such, you simply need to turn off the main circuit breaker to shut down power in the entire house, but you can still have electric power flowing through the wiring installations that are directly connected to your electric meter.

Sub-panels

Sub-panels and secondary circuit breakers are installed in relevant positions within a wiring system. This enhances the distribution of electricity to different outlet points that require varying levels of electrical current. A sub-panel contains its own set of circuit breakers and is mostly used to create some kind of substations for distributing power to specific sections or appliances in your house. For example, you could have a sub-panel for distributing electricity specifically to your laundry room. The sub-panel transmits electrical power to the branch circuits, which in turn, distributes the power to different destinations points.

Unlike the main circuit breaker, which shuts down the entire wiring system, a secondary circuit breaker shuts down the power supply to particular outlets and receptacles within the wiring system. This form of protection allows you to control the flow of electricity to certain appliances without necessarily shutting down the entire system. This flexibility is particularly important during repairs and maintenance.

Circuit Breaker

The circuit breaker provides both manual and automated solutions for electric power controls and protection. It is designed to interrupt or disconnect the flow of electric current, whenever the need arises, both under normal and abnormal conditions. The operation of a circuit breaker under normal conditions involves disruption of current flow by turning it off manually. For example, the circuit breaker is always helpful in cutting off power supply when you need to inspect or repair damages to your wiring system. The automated disruption of the flow of power by a circuit breaker occurs under abnormal conditions, such as sudden power surge. This will protect the power from spreading and damaging your appliances and other electric installations.

There are different types of circuit breakers, including the air magnetic, plain air, oil, and the vacuum circuit breaker, among others. The air magnetic circuit breaker basically runs on air as the powering medium.

This type of circuit breaker consists of several metallic or coated plates lying between the electrodes. If it is the metallic plates that are in use, the striking of the arc brings it in contact with the metal plates, causing it to disintegrate and lowering the voltage. But if the circuit breaker is fitted with insulated plates, the magnetic dynamics will come into play to neutralize the arc. The arc's relevance to the circuit breaker is discussed in greater detail under the "Circuit Breakers Installation" subtitle in chapter three.

The plain air circuit breaker depends on chamber-controlled arc neutralization mechanisms around contacts or electrodes. The chamber that is known as an arc chute is designed to spread a cooling effect. The arc chute basically pulls in the arc and conveys it to a winding exit located on its walls. There are several other compartments and metallic plates with the plain air circuit breaker that initiate cooling mechanisms for neutralizing the arc.

Just as the name suggests, the vacuum circuit breaker cuts off the air supply to dismantle the arc. It is structured on dialectic recovery mechanisms that interrupt the flow of high electric energy current and diffuse or completely to halt the arc's prevalence in between the contacts.

The oil circuit breaker is powered by oil and uses gas decompression mechanisms to extinguish the arc. Its set up has both fixed and movable electrodes dipped in oil, which provide insulating properties to the contacts. The separation of the contacts as a result of electric current flow triggers the vaporization and transformation of the oil into hydrogen gas. The gas neutralizes the ability of the arc to generate repeated strikes.

Electrical Box

An electrical box is the covering that is screwed into the drilled hole of an outlet to provide housing for the wires of your switches, receptacles, and other outlets. The drilled holes for lighting are also covered by electric boxes. Once you have drilled the holes for your receptacles, switches, and lighting, the next step involves pulling the wires through the electric box and screwing the electric box into place.

The electric box actually provides a firm base against which you will screw your switches, receptacles, and other outlets. Most of them will also contain built-in clamps for holding wires firmly in place. Others bear functional designs that you can customize to meet your varying wiring needs. For example, you can expand the size of your electrical box by simply connecting several boxes that have detachable sides. You can apply this expansion technique on both standard and multiple-gang electrical boxes. This will allow you to hold more devices on that particular electrical box.

There are different shapes and sizes of electrical boxes. The widely used single-socket, single-switch, and any other single outlet receptacle are rectangular shaped. Multi-switch and multi-socket electrical boxes, as well as electrical boxes for any other multiple outlet receptacles, are collectively referred to as multi-gang boxes. They are rectangular in shape, as well. Electrical boxes for single-switch and single-outlet receptacles are considered to be the standard size. The measurement of a standard electrical box is 2x3x1.5 inches (HxWxD). There are also some that have longer depths and measure 2x3x3.5 inches (HxWxD). The size of multi-gang electrical boxes varies with the number of devices they can accommodate.

A standard electrical box that is suited for use in housing wire splices is known as a junction box. This is where a 4-inch square electrical box comes in handy. With a measurement of between 1.5 and 2.13 inches, this box provides a spacious room for accommodating multiple connections of wires and cables. The square electrical box is also useful for running multiple wires or cables to multiple directions.

The electrical boxes for lighting fixtures are usually round in shape. Round electrical boxes can be plastic or metallic and exist in standard sizes that range between 1.5 to 3 inches. The plastic option is easier to use because it is designed with protruding ear-like curves for screwing it to the surface. You can also consider using the metallic type, especially if your conduit is mounted on the surface.

The round pan is another notable type of electrical box. This particular type of electrical box is best suited for use in mounting lights on the ceiling or walls. However, performing your electrical manipulations on these boxes can be a bit tricky because of their shallow depth and small size, which ranges between 0.5 to 0.75 inches. You have to be extra cautious when fixing your wires in round electrical boxes to ensure that they fit properly.

There are many other shapes for an electrical box, designed to add aesthetic and sometimes functional value to your wiring system. For example, there are octagon-shaped varieties that are mostly used to mount lights on ceilings and walls. The mounting of a fan on your ceiling also requires special attention when it comes to selecting the appropriate electrical box. You can use either a 2.13-inch standard size round electrical box or a round pan as an alternative. You will have to go for the metallic option if you decide to use the round pan to give the fan a firmer hold. You could alternatively use an octagon-shaped electrical box to mount your fan.

Electrical boxes are also classified according to their design structure and the nature of wiring work that you use with them. This includes new work and old work boxes. You will also encounter electrical boxes that are classified according to their location of installation, such as ceiling boxes. New work, old work, and ceiling work electrical boxes are discussed in greater detail in the next chapter.

There are also solutions for electrical boxes that fall short of the depth measurements required to fit perfectly in your drilled holes. One of these solutions is the use of box extenders or extensions. Instead of struggling to cover your drilled hole to reduce its depth, just insert a box extender of a similar height and width to adjust its depth. The box extender serves this purpose well because it is open on both sides.

Junction Box

As we have already seen in the previous sub-topic, the junction box houses connections for multiple wires or cables. There are various factors you must consider when installing your junction box. For example, you must install the junction box in an open location that is readily accessible. It must also be sealed firmly with a solid cover. The recommended cover thresholds of the electrical box are part of the NEC requirements for safety.

Fittings

Ensure that you have all the relevant fittings for the metallic and non-metallic components and fixtures of your wiring system. Fittings are useful for providing structural support and enhancing the safety of different components and installations in the wiring system. They come in a variety of shapes, sizes, designs, and material compositions, depending on their uses. This ranges from elbows, nipples, strut clamps, connectors, grounding screws, conduit supports, couplings, steel boxes, and straps, among others.

Couplings are useful for linking separate segments of conduit together. You will need threaded coupling to join single pieces or compression coupling to link multiple pieces at a particular point. For example, when you tighten the end of one metallic conduit carrying exposed threads against the corresponding joint of a different conduit segment carrying the internal threads, this is a single-piece coupling. Compression coupling works if you use a locknut to join two separate conduit segments bearing exposed threads. Set-screw coupling, a method that involves the use of screws that are not permanently fixed, is also a viable alternative and is commonly used to join single pieces.

Straps come in handy when attaching conduits to walls and other surfaces, thanks to their u-shape design and screw holes that help hold the conduit firmly. You can alternatively use c-shaped strut clamps bearing two holes on each side. The difference between straps and strut clamps is the former embraces almost the entire circumference of the conduit and may have a single screw hole, while the latter always has two screw holes.

Elbow joints provide the flexibility of changing the direction of the conduit. For example, you may need to fix an elbow at the tip of a vertical conduit to connect it to a horizontal conduit. Apart from elbow joints, conduit bodies are equally important fittings because you can install them as pull boxes or use them to change the direction of conduit segments.

Use fittings correctly all the time to guarantee the safety and structural integrity of your wiring project.

Improper or insufficient use of a fitting is one of the reasons a building inspector may deny you the approval to progress with your project. For example, threaded couplings or glued joints that are loosely held together will compromise the safety of your wiring. This will provide the inspector sufficient grounds for denying you the required approval.

The Conduit

A conduit allows you to secure your electric cables and wires inside either non-metallic or metallic tubings. A conduit is useful in creating structurally sound wiring systems and navigating areas that may be prone to hazards, such as water. You will find it more convenient to organize the running of your cables and to identify their terminal points when using conduits. There are several types of rigid and flexible conduits that you may consider adopting for your wiring project.

You will find a rigid conduit useful for running your cables in straight lines. A rigid metal conduit (RMC) is particularly useful for running cables in exposed locations. Consider using this galvanized steel type RMC for your outdoor wiring project because it is composed of strong materials that are designed to withstand weather elements and other threats that could potentially damage your cables. There is a 20-foot option with threaded ends that is suited for use over longer distances between the terminal points of electric power cables. The 10-foot option provides you greater flexibility for short distances or cabling that requires frequent change of direction.

Electrical metallic tubing (EMT) is the other viable option for both your indoor and outdoor wiring projects. This particular type of conduit is thinner and can be bent with ease, compared to the rigid metal conduit. It is linked using connectors because it does not have threaded ends. That is the reason why the EMT is preferable in exposed indoor wiring. If you choose to use it in your outdoor wiring, ensure that you deploy the appropriate fittings to prevent water from leaking into the tubing. The diameter of the electrical metallic tubing ranges from 0.5 to 1 inch in size.

There is also flexible metal conduit that boasts malleable properties for easy manipulation and change of direction of your cabling. You will find it useful in housing your indoor cables that connect power between source and destination points and are within close proximity to each other. Flexible metal conduit is widely used for cabling that connects specialized appliances to the power source.

Non-metallic conduit, such as plastic conduit, is suited for use in both indoor and outdoor settings. You can easily cut the conduit to different sizes to fit your cabling design. Different pieces are linked using glued fittings, such as elbows and connectors. The non-corrosive nature of PVC and the fact that you can seal all joints tight with glue are the properties that make non-metallic conduit suitable for use in outdoor wiring.

Fuses

Fuses have always been a crucial component of a fuse box breaker. But the gradual preference of circuit breakers over fuse box breakers among home builders has gradually diminished the use of the fuse in electrical installations. The fuse is now mostly included as a built-in component of electrical appliances. However, you are still likely to interact with fuses when renovating an old wiring system that uses a fuse box breaker. The fuse is responsible for cutting off current flow in the event of a sudden power surge, short-circuits, or other types of electrical emergencies. You will probably want to inspect all the fuses in an old house and replace the ones that are damaged to restore your electrical circuits.

Receptacles

Electrical outlets and electrical receptacles are widely used interchangeably to mean the same thing. However, the two are different because an electrical outlet has a broader scope, considering that it describes the access point to an electric system for both receptacle and lighting installations. For example, you have to mount a light fixture on a lighting outlet or an electrical box to connect it to power. A receptacle, on the other hand, describes the electrical system access points strictly on appliances. Therefore, a receptacle is a type of outlet that provides a controlled and safe flow of power from the electrical box to the destination appliances.

The requirements for the installation of receptacles in different rooms of the house are some of the most highlighted areas of electrical code. For example, there are receptacles that are specifically designed for the kitchen or the bathroom, while there are others that can be installed in any part of the house. There are other NEC requirements for receptacles, such as a tamper-proof design that prevents the insertion of foreign objects, especially by children.

Receptacles are mainly classified according to the capacity of their electric current or their functional design. You will most likely be choosing between 120-volt, 120 and 240-volt, and 240-volt options for different receptacle installations. There are also minimum amperage and compatibility requirements for some types of receptacle installations. For example, it is recommended that you limit your home receptacles to 15 amps and 20 amps. But you must remember that, whereas a 20-amp receptacle accepts both 15-amp and 20 amp plugs, a 15-amp receptacle accepts strictly 15-amp plugs. Some of the widely used receptacles fall in the duplex, split, GFCI, and AFCI categories.

A duplex receptacle is created when two single receptacles are collapsed to form one unit. But rather than occupy double electrical box slots, the duplex receptacle is installed on a single box. The duplex receptacle is widely used in home wiring because it provides both structural and functional flexibility. For example, it is possible to install simple and easy-to-implement back wiring on a duplex receptacle if you experience difficulties using the recommended side wiring. A duplex receptacle also contains a detachable metal tab that provides a connection to the terminal screws on each side of the receptacle.

The GFCI, or ground-fault circuit interrupter, is a special type of circuit breaker that disrupts the flow of electric current to protect you from the risk of electrocution. The GFCI is recommended for use in wet areas – such as the bathroom, garage, kitchen, and outdoor locations – because it is designed to maintain extreme sensitivity to water. It provides protection against potential shock in the event of water coming into contact with electricity.

The slightest variation of an electric current is sufficient to trigger the GFCI's instant shut down of the current flow. All other GFCI receptacles connected to the affected receptacle will shut down, as well. You have to manually turn the power back on in the affected circuit using the reset button on the GFCI. Push the reset tab to restore power supply to the GFCI and its corresponding circuits. The GFCI receptacle also contains a test button that you can use to examine its functional state on a frequent basis. You only need to push the test button to see if the receptacle is working.

The AFCI, or arc-fault circuit interrupter, is more or less an advancement of the GFCI because the two operate on almost the same principles. It is uniquely designed to prevent fire by detecting and reacting instantly to electrical arc faults. Such arc faults are caused by faulty or poorly connected electrical wires. The NEC requires that you install AFCI in critical areas that are prone to fire, such as the kitchen.

Chapter Summary

- Safety gear and equipment ranks high among electrical wiring preparation priorities because of the delicate and risk-inherent nature of electricity.
- An electrical system consists of many parts, components, and elements that are combined through wiring to create the delivery and distribution infrastructure of electric power.
- Receptacles that convey power to high-voltage appliances in the kitchen must have GFCI and/or AFCI protection.

In the next chapter, you will learn the nature and scope of tasks involved in indoor wiring.

Chapter Three: Indoor Wiring

Indoor wiring consists of all the wiring operations that you perform inside a building or in a makeshift structure. This may be your main house, a garage, or a building extension. With the exception of the kitchen and bathroom, which require waterproof materials, indoor wiring in the other rooms of a building requires ordinary electrical wiring materials.

Types of Wiring Systems

Concealed conduit wiring should be your priority choice when selecting a wiring system for your home. It is more or less the standard of home wiring systems because it provides greater safety guarantees. Plastic or metallic piping is used to hide conduits in walls, beneath the floor, and in the roof. You have to chisel out channels for laying your conduits on floors and plaster them once you are done with the wiring installation.

Ensure that your conduits run in a continuous pattern and interconnected appropriately to guarantee the uninterrupted flow of electricity. Consider using a PVC conduit because it is cheaper compared to metallic conduit and does not involve demanding safety requirements during installation. However, if you prefer metallic conduit, make sure that it touches the earth at a particular point of the installation layout as a safety measure against electrolytic attacks. But remember that the connection of metallic conduits to earth attracts extra costs, as well. Conduit sizes range from between 0.5 to 2-inches in diameter. Choose your conduit sizes wisely to avoid congesting your cables in a single tube.

You can use either screwed, split, or flexible conduit, depending on whether you are using a non-metallic or a metallic conduit. Screwed conduit is made of firm and protective metallic material and is designed for use in underground wiring. Split conduit exists as parts that are threaded together using pipe joints. It is made up of metallic material, as well, and is meant strictly for use in surface wiring. Flexible conduit may be either metallic or plastic, although the PVC variety is widely used in home wiring. Its flexibility is useful in areas that require bending or resizing of the conduit.

The procedure for surface conduit wiring is similar to that of concealed conduit wiring, save for the manner in which conduits are hooked on the surface. You will most likely find this type of wiring system is useful on the walls and the ceiling. Rather than cutting channels on the walls, as is the case with concealed conduit wiring, you instead chisel holes where you will install wall plugs for holding the conduits in position.

Although conduit wiring, whether concealed or surface, has many advantages, it presents some drawbacks associated with the cost and structural aspects of the wiring system. For example, you will pay more when using PVC or metallic conduits, compared to materials used in alternative wiring systems. Moreover, a lot of work is involved in the installation and it is difficult to detect defects when they occur in the cables inside the conduits. Conduit wiring also limits your flexibility to expand and customize the wiring system in the future.

A batten wiring system is the other option at your disposal and it offers the single-core, double-core, and triple-core cable varieties. These batten wiring varieties may take the form of tough rubber sheathed (TRS) or cab tyre sheathed (CTS) cabling. TRS cables are known to be resistant to water and chemicals when used indoors. Its installation is simple because you only need to use buckle clips to attach the cables on a straight wooden surface. The buckle clips should be fixed at evenly spaced intervals on both the vertical and horizontal runs to secure the cables firmly against the surface. The recommended distance for vertical and horizontal runs is 10cm and 15cm, respectively.

The batten wiring system provides advantages, such as ease of future customizations, decent appearance, durability, and safety. However, it has some downsides, as well, including fire risks, limitations to a maximum wattage of 250V, and lack of resistance to weather elements in outdoor locations. Therefore, this wiring system is not suitable for outdoor wiring.

Casing capping and cleat wiring are the other wiring types you may consider for your upgrade or new projects. In casing capping wiring, you place your insulated wires in either grey or cap-covered plastic casing. The bedding is screwed to the wall and the wires are concealed by the top cover once the wiring has been completed. Casing capping wiring is more convenient and durable compared to wooden casing capping that was widely used in the past.

Cost savings is the main advantage associated with casing capping wiring. You can also opt for this type of wiring system in rooms you have partitioned with delicate materials or skinny walls. In fact, casing capping wiring is widely used in office partitions with skinny walls that cannot conceal conduits. The plastic casing is durable and provides you the flexibility to have separate installations for the live and neutral wires. Casing capping also has impressive safety thresholds because it protects wires and cables from damage by weather and other elements.

Cleat wiring, on the other hand, involves mounting braided insulated electric wire on open or exposed surfaces, such as walls. It is a simple form of wiring because it does not involve the deployment of conduits or drilling of raceways. Porcelain cleats are all that is needed to hold the braided wires to walls and other surfaces. Cleat wiring is cost-effective and makes for easy inspection and detection of damaged or faulty sections.

Cleat wiring is the kind of system you will need to consider for a temporary structure because of its high exposure to risks, such as electric shock. Having exposed wires on your walls is not something you will want to entertain, especially if you have kids in the house. It will also be tricky to maintain such a cleat wiring system in wet environments. Having cleat wiring in your kitchen or bathroom is suicidal. It also lacks that touch that you will want in your home finishing.

Rough-In Wiring
Reaching the rough-in stage in wiring means you have completed all the essential aspects of laying and connecting wires and cables, as well as installing all the necessary components. At this point, you should have completed most of the fundamental aspects of wiring infrastructure, including drilling channels, concealing or nailing conduits, pulling cables through conduits, and installing electrical boxes and panels. You are only waiting for the building inspector's approval before wrapping up the operation.

The floor, wall, and ceiling installation of your rough-in wiring layout must remain open. You will only be able to cover the system after approval by the building inspector. This makes it easier for the building inspector to scrutinize the wiring and either approve or reject it. It also provides you the convenience of implementing any modifications that your building inspector might suggest. The installation of fixtures, such as receptacles, switches, and lighting, happens after the approval of the rough-in wiring.

Remember that rough-in is not an experimental exercise - it is the final implementation of your wiring system. You will most likely fall in trouble with your building inspector if you approach the rough-in phase as a work-in-progress that you will keep modifying. Therefore, you must do a thorough job to earn your building inspector's approval. The best approach to this is to use the recommended quality of materials and observe the provisions of the NEC regulations.

Requisite Materials

Some of the materials you will need for your indoor rough-in wiring include cables (preferably the NM cable), wire connectors, plastic electrical boxes, and odds and ends. Feel free to add other materials of your choosing, depending on your desired customizations. The materials listed above are simply the ones you will always need in any type of indoor wiring project.

Choose either three-conductor or four-conductor cable for convenience purposes, especially when you need to connect three-way switches at some point. Plastic boxes are preferable because they are less expensive and provide greater flexibility, compared to metallic electrical boxes. The recommended minimum size of electrical box – that is, the 18 cubic-inch or the 20.25 cubic-inch, will suffice for the installation of single switches and receptacles. Select matching boxes for multiple-switch outlets. Remember that the boxes for your light fixtures are always rounded. But since you are bound to experience challenges fixing round electrical boxes in certain sections of the house, such as joists, you will find bar hangers useful in overcoming such problems.

There are several color varieties of wire connectors that you can choose from. They are packaged in boxes, each containing red, green, or yellow connectors. The red and yellow wire connectors are the ones that are widely used in home electrical wiring. But there are occasions where an inspector may recommend that you use green wire connectors on the ground of technicalities or any other requirements.

Consider buying other miscellaneous materials, such as staples, electrical tape, and nail plates. You will need these materials to mark cables or cover stripped cables. Staples will be particularly useful in holding your cables firmly in place. Metal nail plates are also useful in the protection of cables.

Rough-In Wiring Implementation

It is always recommended to have a task schedule before beginning work on your home wiring project. This will allow you to track and complete all the required tasks and installations required for a particular stage before proceeding to the next stage. Leaving gaps for later is a risky approach because you may end up with issues, such as unconnected terminals, exposed outlets for receptacles, or hazardously hanging wires for lighting.

Electrical Box Installation

By now, you should have decided on the number of electrical boxes you want to install and their specific locations. If you are installing your electrical system in a new house that is under construction, the process will be a bit easier because you will complete your wiring installations on the studs before fixing the drywall. But if you are fixing the electrical system in an old house, you will need to use the stud finder to locate the studs where you will install your electrical boxes. To install an electrical box is a simple procedure that involves the steps below:

- Step one: Measure the space between the edges and the center of each box. Mark the central points of the boxes while making the measurements.
- Step two: Give each box a unique identification according to its purpose and its targeted installation location. You can use letters, symbols, or a combination of both to tag the identification marks on the boxes.
- Step three: Use symbols to map out the different outlets and their locations on the studs. This will include the symbols for switches, receptacles, and light fixtures. The symbols should also indicate the type of switches in you will be installing both single switches and double or three-way switches.
- Step four: Set the height level for each of your switches and outlets. The recommended height of a switch and an outlet from the floor is 48 inches and 12 inches, respectively.
- Step five: Screw the electrical box at a depth that will be aligned with the drywall once it is put

back. The thickness between the wall or the studs and the drywall usually averages 0.5 inches. That should be the average margin margins that you should allow, so as to provide room for the drywall adjustments.

Computing Electrical Box Size

NEC regulations impose limitations on the maximum number of wires you can have in a single electrical box. You will experience more convenience if you use plastic boxes because most have the details of their wire accommodation capacities embossed inside. For metallic boxes, you will have to refer to the specific details from the NEC.

However, you can still go a step further and compute your own estimation of the size of electrical boxes you will require for your wiring. This computation is based on mainly the functional aspects of the different wire. A simple computation involves getting the sum of the number of functionally diverse wires that you will accommodate in a particular electrical box. For example, for an electrical box connection consisting of live and neutral wires, a combination of ground wires, and a combination of cable clamping material, as well as the switch and outlet components, you will add one for each of the first three items and add two for the fourth item. This will give you a total sum of nine because there will be two live-wire and one neutral-wire terminals, as well as four-wire terminals for the switches and outlets. Add one each for the ground wire and cable clamping combinations and you get nine.

At this point, the size of your electrical box will be dictated by the quantity and size of your wires. If you are using 12-gauge wire, you will multiply 9 by 2.25 to determine the minimum cubic-inch size for the box. But if you are using 14-gauge wire, you will multiply 9 by 2 to determine the minimum cubic-inch size for your electrical box. The computation of the minimum sizes for the two boxes will be 18 cubic inches and 20.25 cubic inches, respectively.

Running Cable
Your wiring project is now gradually taking shape and you have reached the stage where you need to run cables to establish a connection between the service panel

and outlet points. This process will involve cutting through the drywall to create spaces and channels for laying your cables.

Start by marking a straight line between the source and destination points of the power flow. Use a saw, or any other appropriate tool of your liking, to cut out the drywall along the line. Do not open up unnecessarily wide spaces in the drywall that will require a lot of effort to fill them back. If you are digging out a plastered wall, use a chisel and a hammer and ensure you limit the width of the vertical or horizontal lines to slightly above the diameter of your conduit. A channel that is slightly bigger than the conduit diameter is recommended for a plastered wall, as it helps hold the conduits firmly in position.

A height of 12 inches is considered sufficient for a horizontal run on drywall because you need a bit of room to maneuver your hands inside the channel. The horizontal run may cut across several studs, depending on the distance between the source and destination of power. Drilling vertical runs is quite different because you need to locate the studs against which you will lay your conduit. You will have to deploy appropriate tools or techniques, such as a stud finder, to determine the actual location of different studs.

Select a suitable auger or spade bit to mount on your drill that to dig holes in the studs. For example, a 0.5-inch spade bit is suitable for drilling holes for 12-gauge wire, while a 0.38-inch spade bit is suitable for drilling holes for 14-gauge wire. The idea behind the recommended spade bit sizes is to ensure that the holes are large enough to fit wires. Too large holes are not recommended because they will weaken the stud, while extremely small holes will make it difficult for you to pull the wires.

Mark the spots for drilling holes in the studs and proceed to drill the holes. Make sure you are drilling right in the middle of the studs. Avoid drilling closer to the face of the stud unless it is extremely necessary. Also, use nail plate protection when drilling holes on sensitive parts of the stud. Be cautious when drilling holes on joists - it is recommended that you drill the holes towards the tips rather than the middle of the joists. The holes must be centered in whatever location you choose to drill toward the tips of the joists.

Proceed to pull your wires through the studs to connect to the designated source and destination points of electric power. This should be an extremely swift procedure, especially if you drilled the holes in a straight line along the studs. In other words, the holes that you drill in the studs should have a similar distance between the floor and the drilling point to simplify the process of pulling cables through the walls. There are also other cautious measures you should take when pulling cables. For example, unravel the cable coil well in advance if you are pulling the cables over long runs to avoid tightening and overstretching the cable. Do not tighten the cable between studs as well - a bit of slack is needed to provide flexibility during the insulation of the wall. Leave a few extra inches at the outlet terminals of the cables because there are occasions when you may need to adjust your electrical boxes.

Take your nail guard plates and fix them over the stud edges to provide protection to both the holes and the cable runs. Crosscheck all the points of your cable runs to ensure that they meet all the NEC requirements. This should mark the end of the rough-in wiring stage and you can proceed to invite your home building inspector to approve your project. Follow the inspector's instructions to modify any parts of your wiring in the event that your wiring project falls short of some requirements.

Sealing and patching the drywall will be the last step you will perform in cabling runs before you proceed to install fixtures for the outlets in the electrical boxes. You may want to put some insulation in your wall before fixing the drywall back into position. Just make sure that there is a bit of slack in the cables between the studs to avoid exposing your cable to tension.

Service Panel Installation

The installation of a service or main panel is an extremely sensitive and dangerous process. It requires caution, even for the most experienced electrician. But that does not mean that you cannot attempt it. You just need to follow the laid out instructions and observe the corresponding building code requirements to install your main panel safely.

Select a main panel size that is appropriate for your house. The size of the main panel is measured in terms of the maximum amps it can carry at a time. Locate the amperage details of the main panel on the inscribed label on the main circuit breaker. You will ideally be looking at an amperage level that is sufficient to power your home. Consider a minimum of 100 amps for your main panel installation because anything lower than that will cripple your home power supply. You could probably go a bit higher, to 150 amps or 200 amps, if you are looking to have stable and sufficient power supplied to the different electrical installations at all times. The problem with a low-amperage main panel is the high frequency of tripping every other time the load of your installations exceeds the panel's maximum amperage capacity.

The initial stage of panel installation must be done in consultation with your power provider. Considering that the service panel is the entry and distribution point of electricity into your house, your power provider will be interested in ensuring that the electric meter is properly installed and connected. Once you are ready to begin the installation, coordinate with your utility company to get them to shut down the power of the main feeder wire.

Using a chisel, remove the loosely attached metal knockouts on the top of the service panel to create gateways for running the main service conduit into the box. You can also use this opportunity to knock off all the other metal knockouts, as well, because you will still need to clear them sooner or later to create entry and exit paths for other cables. The service panel has different sizes of metal knockouts around it and this helps you determine the entry or exit points of the different sizes of conduit and cables. The knockouts for the main feeder conduit are always the largest.

Take your cable connectors and fix each one of them into their prescribed locations inside the panel. This is an easy process because you only need to use lock nuts to thread the cable connectors into the panel.

Select an appropriate service panel location close to the point where the main feeder cable has been connected to your house. This provides you with the convenience of establishing a connection between your service panel and the metal conduit on which the main service cable rests. Hold the service panel in position to ensure that it is aligned to the main service conduit and that all the screw holes are aligned to the studs. You need to attach the panel to the studs for it to hold firmly. Insert and tighten the screws until the panel is mounted firmly against the wall.

Proceed to ground your panel and all its associated circuits to enhance the safety of your wiring system. Attach the ground wire to the panel's grounding connector and run it right into the ground using a bare wire. You can use a plastic or metallic conduit and corresponding screw clamps to hold the ground wire firmly to the ground. The ground wire does not pose risks when attached to the ground because it always has zero voltage.

Direct your focus toward establishing a connection between the service wires in the panel and the main service conduit. The fish tape tool for pulling wires through conduit will be instrumental at this stage of service panel installation. The idea here is to hook and pull the main service wires inside the main service conduit downward to the panel. To perform this task, drive the fish tape upwards through the conduit-designated hole on the top part of the panel. Use electric tape to hook the fish tape to the service wires and gently pull it down to the service panel. Pull wires that are long enough to reach any part of the service panel for ease of connections.

Strip the insulation at the top-most tips of the two main service black wires. The stripping should not stretch that much along the length of the wires to avoid leaving too much wire naked after they are inserted and screwed to their destination circuit breaker terminals. Having bare or exposed wiring in the service panel will compromise its safety thresholds.

Slant the two main service wires at an angle of about 90 degrees and insert them to the service panel's topmost circuit breaker, which actually is the main breaker. The main breaker is always at the top of the chain of breakers in a service panel, while the subsidiary breakers occupy the lower segments. Like I discussed earlier in chapter two, the main breaker controls the supply of power to the entire house. It is a 240-volt service panel component that connects to the other circuit breakers through the two hot bus bars that stretch the panel's entire height.

Now that the bare tips of the main service wires are safely attached to the lug terminals of the main breaker, proceed and tighten the screws to secure them firmly. Proceed to establish a connection between the neutral wire of the main service conduit and the panel's neutral bus bar. At this point, you will have completed connecting the service panel power inlet to the main service conduit and its wires. But the process is not complete because you need to connect the service panel to its subsidiary electric power distribution channels.

Take your fish tape again, insert it through the designated hole of a particular branch or subsidiary circuit to the conduit housing the wires. Hook the fish tape to the wires with electrical tape and gently pull the excess wires into the service panel. This will afford you flexibility during the installation of the wires to any part of the panel. However, you will not need to use fish tape if the wires of the branch circuits are not contained in the conduit.

Remove the insulation from the tips of the cables to expose only a small portion of the wires. Again, remember the stripping of the tips should be as minimal as possible to avoid having visible stretches of bare wire in the panel. Install connectors into the panel, insert the wires into the connectors, and tighten the screws to hold the wires firmly in place.

Connect the hot wires of the branch circuits to the lugs in their respective branch breakers in the panel. Tighten the screws to hold the wires firmly in place. Direct all the bare ground wires and the neutral wires of the branch circuits to the ground bus bar and neutral bus bar, respectively. This is effectively the last step of the service panel installation. You can now use loops to attach the excess cables to the sides of the panel.

There are a few points you need to keep in mind when connecting the wires of the subsidiary or branch circuits to the respective lugs in the service panel. For example, you have to ensure that insert wires of the recommended sizes and amperage to the lugs of the branch circuits. That is because each of the different branch circuits in the panel is designed for a specific function.

Sub-panel Installation

The installation of the sub-panel is similar to that of the main panel, except for the source and destination points of electric power flow. A sub-panel draws its power from the main panel before distributing it to specific locations within the house to be distributed to specific outlets for different appliances. Simply follow the same procedure as that of the service panel when installing the sub-panel. Remember to use sub-panels that are well suited for their particular purposes, in terms of current, voltage, and wire-size specifications.

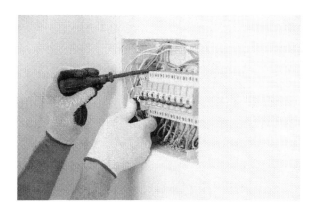

Circuit Breaker Installation

Before getting down to the business of installing a circuit breaker, let us explore how it works and understand its operational dynamics. Movable and fixed electrodes are the basic components of a circuit breaker.

These electrodes remain closed under normal conditions and open only when abnormal conditions arise or when the circuit breaker is manually switched off. Under abnormal conditions, the sudden occurrence of a fault in the electrical system triggers panic mechanisms that automatically open the electrodes. The panic mechanisms that trigger the automatic opening of the electrodes actually originate from the flow of energy to the trip coil, which in turn separates the contacts or electrodes.

Crosscheck to ensure that your circuit breaker contains the appropriate ratings for specific wire types and designated circuit loads. For example, a 15-amp breaker is appropriate for receptacle installations, while a 20-amp breaker is best suited for lighting. Also, remember that a single slot is sufficient for a breaker that is powered by circuits transmitting 120 volts of electric current. Breakers powered by circuits transmitting 240 volts of electric current, on the other hand, require double slots.

The rest of the steps for installing a circuit breaker are similar to the installation of the sub-panel. The only difference is the source and destination points of the electric power flow. You have to connect the line wires of each circuit breaker to the designated lugs in the main panel and distribute the power to the corresponding circuits.

The Arc Phenomenon

You need a bit of knowledge of the arc phenomenon to understand the potential hindrances to the operating mechanisms of the electrodes or contacts of the circuit breaker. An arc is a form of electrical force that prevails between electrodes the moment they are automatically separated in response to the emergence of a fault in the electrical system. Normally, the circuit's current flow will remain uninterrupted until that point when the arc is neutralized.

The significance of this arc phenomenon is that it harbors the potential to cause serious damage. Such damage is common during events like electrical power surges and short-circuiting. This is because the arc's prevalence may inhibit the automated separation of the electrodes. The arc also generates a lot of heat that could damage the circuit breaker and spread to other components within the system. The heat results from the sudden compression of the contact area during the opening of the electrodes. This is followed by the sudden escalation of the power density, due to the large current emanating from the short circuit. The temperatures soar to alarming levels, thereby ionizing the medium – usually air or oil - and transforming it into a conductor, effectively creating an arc between the electrodes. That means the open electrodes will experience deflated resistance between them and that will cause the electric current to continue flowing and rendering the circuit breaker redundant.

Therefore, as you go about the business of installing a circuit breaker, keep in mind that you will have to deploy relevant measures to protect your circuit breaker from arc phenomenon attacks. Gaps between contacts or electrodes and the presence of ionized elements between the electrodes are considered to be the primary causes of the arc phenomenon. This is where you should direct your focus when exploring measures of dismantling the arc.

High resistance and low resistance methods are the widely recommended solutions to curbing the arcs or preventing their occurrence. In the high-resistance method, you will be looking at expanding resistance to the arc to dissolve the current to levels that cannot sustain an arc. You can deploy this method through a variety of measures that include stretching the arc length and suppressing the arc's cross-section area. You can also split or reduce the arc's temperature. However, you will most likely find this method when dealing with DC rather than AC circuit breakers because of the unusually high levels of heat that the arc-dilution process generates. You will still find this method useful in solar-powered connections and other processes that involve DC to AC power transformation.

This leaves you with the low resistance method, which involves diluting the resistance levels of the arc to extremely low levels that will render them insignificant. The low resistance method is well suited for an AC circuit breaker because it cripples the arc's ability to keep striking whenever there is an increase of voltage between the electrodes.

Having dealt with the issue of differences or gaps between electrodes, you can now shift your attention to the issue of ionization of the medium. The strategy here will be to seek mechanisms for the deionization of the space between the electrodes at faster rates than the rates at which the ionization occurs. This will impair the arc's ability to generate repeated strikes wherever there are spikes in the levels of the ionized medium. Some of the recommended solutions here will be to stretch the gaps of the electrodes and expand the pressure, as well. You can also deploy cooling mechanisms to reduce the temperatures between the contacts.

Receptacle Installation

The approval of your rough-in wiring sets the stage for you to complete your wiring project. You now need to install receptacles, lighting, and other outlets to the electrical boxes that you attached to different locations in the house.

But before we dive into the details of receptacle installation, let us have a brief overview of the architecture and wiring structure of a receptacle. One of the conspicuous features of a receptacle is the positioning of its ground pin at the bottom, rather than the top. The brass-colored hot terminal, the silver-colored neutral terminal, and the green-colored ground terminal are the other highlight features of the architecture of a receptacle.

The coloring makes it easier for you to attach the different wires to their respective terminals. This helps you avoid the short circuit risks associated with the wrong installation of service line wires to the receptacle terminals. Terminal screws are used to hold the wires firmly in place.

The other standard feature of a receptacle is the presence of a flexible metal tab that provides a connection to the terminal screws on each side of the receptacle. You can create a barrier between the terminals by simply removing the metal tab.

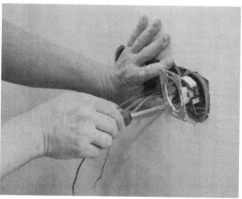

Different types of receptacles bear different terminal designs. For example, there is the screw type of terminal that is common in receptacles. This particular type of terminal allows you to bend the tip of the wire into a c-shaped curve, wrapping it around a terminal and tightening the screw to hold it in position. You will most likely interact with the slightly different slide-in terminal in the GFCI and other receptacles. This type of receptacle involves stripping the tip of the wire and sliding it right under the terminal screw. The shove in, or push-in terminal, also involves stripping the tip of the wires, but does not require the wires to be screwed. The wires are held into position in the terminal hole by a firm grip. These structural differences show that you will always encounter surprises when interacting with different types of electrical installations.

The wiring structure of the receptacle consists of two non-metallic cables that connect the electrical box of the first receptacle to an electrical panel or circuit. The black or hot wire is connected to the receptacle terminals alongside the neutral wire. The usual procedures for the ground wire to the device ground terminal connection in the outlet box are applied to the ground wires. This means that a connection is created among all the ground wires and between the ground wires and their corresponding ground terminals in the devices. There are two exit NM wires that establish a connection with the next receptacle in the chain. This interconnection pattern is maintained to the final receptacle in the chain.

The installation of the receptacle to an electrical box is not a complex procedure because the terminal destinations for different wires are clearly marked. It is as easy as connecting a lighting switch. Strip the tips of the line, neutral, and ground wire. Insert the line, neutral, and ground wires of the electrical box to the brass, silver, and green terminals of the receptacle, respectively. Screw the wires tight on the receptacles to hold them firm inside the terminals. Mount the receptacle on the electrical box and screw it tight into position. Place the receptacle cover to complete the process. Once you complete all other installations, use a receptacle tester to verify if your newly installed receptacles are working.

Chapter Summary

- Concealed conduit wiring is widely used for indoor wiring because it does not compromise safety in the house, compared to surface wiring.
- Rough-in wiring is the actual but incomplete layout of different electrical components and installations in the house.
- The arc phenomenon must be eliminated from the electrical circuit breaker because it can potentially cause a fire.

In the next chapter, you will learn the procedures for implementing different outdoor wiring projects.

Chapter Four: Outdoor Wiring

Outdoor wiring concerns all installations that are exterior to your house. This includes wiring for installations such as security lighting, swimming pools, and path lamps, among others.

We have already covered the materials and equipment you require to perform your electrical wiring operations efficiently. Some of these materials and equipment can be used across the board, while others are restricted to either indoor or outdoor wiring. Unlike indoor wiring, outdoor wiring requires materials that have been strengthened or customized to withstand exposure to weather and other types of elements. Ensure that your designated materials for use in your DIY outdoor wiring project meet all the recommended thresholds. Some of the uniquely designed items for outdoor wiring include buried cables and outdoor electrical boxes, among others.

For example, an outdoor electrical box performs similar functions as an indoor electrical box, the only difference being their design and material composition. The design of an outdoor electrical box is actually customized for use with outdoor fixtures and outlets. It is constructed from water-resistant materials suitable for use in wet conditions. PVC and aluminum are the widely used materials for an outdoor electrical box because of their high levels of resistance to weather elements. You must seal the boxes tightly because any leakages will compromise the core aspects of your outdoor wiring system.

We will not dwell upon the specifics of the materials and equipment of outdoor wiring to avoid repetition of some of the details that are stated already in the first three chapters of this book. Instead, this book will highlight the specific unique attributes or structure of different outdoor equipment in the course of the overall discussion of outdoor wiring.

Outdoor Wiring Codes
Outdoor wiring is subject to NEC provisions and you must refer to the appropriate requirements when making your electrical installations. Issues of safety are particularly of paramount importance because of the exposed nature of the components of the outdoor wiring infrastructure.

Outdoor Receptacle Code
There are several NEC requirements to look out for during the installation of outdoor receptacles. These requirements concern outlet installations for outdoor locations attached to the house, such as balconies, and those that are completely detached from the house. For example, you are required to use weather resistance-rated

and weatherproof covered receptacles in exposed, damp, or wet locations. And you will have to install receptacles to your deck or balcony if its measurement exceeds 20 square feet.

Install a grade-accessible receptacle at the front and back of your house at a maximum height of 6.5 feet, according to NEC requirements. You will also require in-use covers for 15-amp or 20-amp receptacles installed in locations that experience wet conditions. GFCI protection is a compulsory requirement for all outdoor electrical installations, with the exception of deicing equipment. The GFCI protection exception is also granted for receptacles that are concealed or beyond reach.

Install a GFCI-protected receptacle for your swimming pool or spa at distances of between 6 and 20 feet from the pool or spa edge. The location of the receptacle should not exceed a height of 6.5 feet, according to NEC requirements. The NEC further requires that you position the ancillary non-GFCI protection equipment for the swimming pool or the spa, such as the power pump, at a minimum distance of 10 feet from the edge of the facility. But if the ancillary equipment has GFCI protection installed, you can have them a bit closer, at a minimum of 6 feet from the inside walls of the facility.

Outdoor Cabling Code

The firm insulation of the NM cable used in indoor wiring should not tempt you into believing that it can be used in outdoor wiring. It is not suited for outdoor use at all. Instead, you should consider using the widely recommended UF cable that is known to bear weather resilient properties suited for outdoor use in residential environments. The one outstanding advantage of UF cable is that you can lay it in underground trenches without using a conduit. As such, both your cable and conduit of choice must pass the required safety and resilience thresholds to be considered safe for use in outdoor wiring.

The NEC requires that any exposed or concealed cable used in outdoor locations must comply with the acceptable thresholds for transmitting electrical power. For example, the minimum recommended depth for a directly buried UF cable is 24 inches. This requirement is meant to provide protection against the accidental exposure of this particular non-metallic cable because it is not protected inside a conduit. However, the recommended depth reduces marginally to 18 inches if you are using a PVC conduit. And if you are using a metallic conduit, such as RMC, you are required to provide a minimum of 6 inches of depth. Low-voltage wiring with a transmission capacity exceeding 30 volts similarly requires a 6-inch minimum depth.

When burying your conduit or cables, it is recommended that you remove all the rocks from the soil so that you are left with a lighter material. This is meant to protect the cables or conduit from the weight of the rocks that could over time eventually compromise their safety. The other key factor to consider, as per the NEC provisions, is the transition of the buried conduit from the source terminals of power to the ground and from the ground to the destination terminals. It is recommended that you maintain the conduit run all the way to the source and destination points.

Outdoor Lighting Code

This code summarizes the guidelines for installing protected lighting fixtures that can withstand wet or damp conditions. For example, the code requires that all lighting fixtures intended for use in wet or damp areas must be prescribed for use in each of those locations. It is also recommended that you deploy watertight or weatherproof-rated electrical boxes for your light fixture installations.

The minimum allowable distance between the swimming pool or spa and your low-voltage lighting fixture installations is 5 feet. Ensure that low-voltage lighting fixtures bear the approval of the authorized testing institutions. Approval is required for either the state of a lighting fixture as a complete system or as a composition of multiple components.

It is important to select an accessible location when mounting your low-voltage lighting transformer. You should also maintain a minimum distance of 5 feet from the outer walls of your swimming pool or spa when selecting the appropriate location for the light switches for either of the facility. This requirement will be an exception if there is a wall separation between the switches and the pool or spa. For example, if the switches are located inside a poolside building, then the requirement won't apply. Also, remember that GFCI protection requirements for outdoor locations are not applicable to lighting installations.

Grounding Wire Connection

Outdoor electrical wiring and installations are always exposed to a variety of destructive elements, including lightning strikes and physical damage. It is for this reason that the ground wire connection is considered to be one of the most important safety features of outdoor wiring circuits. The grounding wire actually allows you to protect your wiring system from the potential risk of a lightning strike or destructive short circuit. It serves the primary purpose of neutralizing the sudden surge of electric current by diverting and driving the excess current to the ground. The grounding wire is one of the priority safety thresholds that you must meet before your wiring is approved by your building inspector.

Design and Layout

Your design and layout considerations for outdoor wiring should focus on the uses and types of facilities or equipment. You need to customize your design to suit the varied requirements for wiring outdoor facilities, such as swimming pools and spas, as well as security and path lighting.

Your outdoor wiring layout begins right from your deck or balcony, if you have one on your house. It is common practice to install balcony lighting as an extension of the interior wiring of the house and installing the lighting switch inside the house, as well. However, the same cannot be said of receptacle installations on your deck or balcony. You have to install and operate such receptacles from the balcony. This means that the receptacles must be secured appropriately with GFCI because they will be exposed to weather elements, including water, rain, and the sun, like any other outdoor electrical installation. It is for these reasons that you must comply with NEC codes for outdoor wiring in your design and layout of the wiring system in your balcony.

Running Outdoor Wiring for a Swimming Pool Pump

Metallic conduit provides the easiest and most convenient option for running cables for outdoor wiring.

This is because it does not require deeper trenches, like non-metallic conduit. However, you can only enjoy this convenience if you are able to meet the extra cost of metallic conduit compared to the non-metallic option. The procedure for running and connecting outdoor wiring in this guide is to use non-metallic or PVC conduit because it is the widely used option in outdoor wiring.

This guide assumes that you have performed all the preliminary requirements and secured the relevant regulatory approval from your local authority to dig up trenches in your compound. Just like indoor wiring, this will be a rough-in kind of wiring that will require your building inspector's approval before you complete the process. If you are unsure about performing certain wiring tasks, such as creating a dedicated circuit, do not hesitate to seek the help of an electrical technician to avoid the trial and error that will expose you to risks.

The first step is to ensure that you have all the customized materials and the specialized tools and equipment that you need to install the outdoor wiring. This should include all the fittings, receptacles, conduit, cables, electrical boxes, elbow joints, connectors, and junction boxes, among others. Also make sure you have fish tape, electric tape, glue, a hammer, screwdriver, drill, auger bits, a backhoe, and a tester.

Identify the nearest source of power in your house, or any other nearby location, relative to your preferred path to the destination point of the wiring. Make sure that your chosen power source is protected by the GFCI receptacle if you do not intend to install a receptacle at the destination point. If you do not have a GFCI-protected point nearby, you can install one by replacing an ordinary outlet with a GFCI receptacle. You could also mount a new GFCI receptacle on the outer wall of your house and establish a connection to a power source inside the house. But for this example, we do not need a GFCI receptacle connection because we will be connecting one at the destination point. The advantage of this format is the convenience of turning the receptacle back on at the destination point in event of power tripping, instead of going all the way to the source point.

Use markings to map a straight path for your conduit between the source and destination points of electric power. You can alternatively hammer metal bars to the ground at each of the two ends and tie a polythene rope between the two bars, so you can dig a straight trench along the rope. Try to avoid barriers, such as paved walkways, as much as possible when creating the path for digging your trench. This will save you the time and effort required to overcome such barriers.

Dig an 18-inch deep trench between the two points as per the NEC recommendations. If you were not able to avoid walkways, or any other barrier, be innovative and find a way across it. For example, dig your trench on both sides of the walkway and, using a sledgehammer, knock a cylindrical-shaped metallic bar from one side of the trench until it crosses underneath the walkway to the other side. The metal bar should be slightly larger than the diameter of your PVC conduit. Pull out the metal bar from under the walkway to create a narrow passage cutting through the underneath of the walkway. You will now be able to lay your conduit and snake it through the narrow passage.

Mount the outdoor electrical box in place at the selected location on the post outlet, using the recommended height specifications of the NEC. This will be ideally the 8 inches or so required to accommodate the recommended minimum distance of the conduit from the ground to the entry point of the destination terminals. This electrical box will be the destination point of power. As such, the conduit will come from the ground right into the outdoor electrical box.

Use elbow joints to connect the horizontal conduit to the vertical conduits at both ends. Since you are using the PVC conduit, you need to seal the connectors tightly with glue to secure it from the underground wet and damp conditions. Lay your conduit from one end of the trench to the other.

Go to the power source and mount a sub-panel close to the exit point of the power. Strip the tips of the line and neutral wires. Connect the line wires of the power exit point to the lugs in the sub-panel. Tighten both screws to hold the wires in place.

Measure the distance from the exit point to the bottom of the trench. Apply the same measurement on the vertical part of the conduit and cut it to size, while leaving the cables that you will attach the exit point hanging by a few inches. Strip off the insulation at the tips of the line, neutral, and ground wires. Hook the wires on a fish tape and pull them close to the exit point. Install connectors into the panel, insert the line wires into the connectors, and tighten the screws to hold the wires firmly in place. Attach the ground and the neutral wires to their respective bus bars in the sub-panel.

Go to the destination point of the power and measure the distance from the entry point to the bottom of the trench. Apply the same measurement on the vertical part of the conduit and cut it to size, while leaving the cables that you will attach the entry point hanging by a few inches. Use a stripper to strip off the insulation at the tips of the line, neutral, and ground wires. Hook the wires on a fish tape and pull them to the inside of the electric box. Connect the wires to their respective terminals in the electrical box.

You will effectively have completed the rough-in wiring version of your outdoor wiring and you can now seek the building inspector's approval. The final steps will involve covering the soil, connecting the GFCI receptacle to the electrical box, and mounting the receptacle cover. You can now plug in your swimming pool pump.

Outdoor Low-Voltage Lighting
Low-voltage lighting mainly features LED fixtures for low dim lighting and low electricity consumption. Installing such lighting in your outdoor spaces saves energy but also creates a unique ambiance in your walk paths, garden, swimming pool area, and the overall appearance of your compound. You need to have a meticulous plan in place to be able to achieve the desired layout and design for your outdoor low-voltage lighting installations. Mapping the layout of your wiring runs will be the best place to start.

Sketch diagrams of your wire runs between the transformer and the different locations in your compound. For example, the series layout is ideal for a simple straight line wire run with lamp posts located in between. A split wire run will suffice if you need to install multiple series lines heading in different directions. A loop wire run is a type of series run that forms a full circle. The layout plan of your wire runs will absolutely depend on the location of your house and the target destination of the wire runs.

The location of the lamp posts is also an important consideration during the planning phase. Space lamp posts farther away from each other if you want to achieve a dim lighting effect. Brightly lit walk paths will require closer gaps between lamp posts.

Before you begin the installation process, ensure you have all the requisite weatherproof equipment and materials designed for use in outdoor wiring. This includes the transformer, conduit, cables, connectors, clamps, lamp posts, and lamps. The choice of wire sizes relative to the distance of the wire runs is extremely important. High-gauge wire is recommended for use over short distances, while low-gauge wire size is recommended for use over longer distances. For example, 14-gauge wire is best suited for distances of up to 78 feet, while 8-gauge wire is best suited for distances over 250 feet.

Remember to seek the necessary approval from your local authority because it is illegal to implement any major wiring project without it. Approval is particularly important for this project because it involves digging trenches.

Installation and Wiring Process
Use a white powder marker to map out the path where your wire runs will lay. Also, mark the areas where you will erect the transformer post and the lamp posts. Dig holes from the points where you will fix the transformer and lamp posts - dig the holes to depths that will be enough to firmly hold the posts in place. Use a backhoe, or any other relevant tool, to dig a trench along the marked path. The trench should be about 18 inches

deep for PVC conduit and 6 inches deep for metallic conduit.

Insert the transformer and lamp posts into their respective holes. Return the soil to the lamp post for the transformer to hold it firmly in position. The soil covering for the post should not go above the trench level because you are yet to lay your conduit. There are some types of outdoor lamps that do not require lamp posts because they are mounted close to ground level. Such outdoor lamps are attached to small chisel-like stakes that are driven into the ground using a mallet hammer. You can also attach them on outside walls or screw them on the side of the pavement.

Mount the transformer to the transformer post at a minimum height of 12 inches. Connect the line wires of the power source in the house to the transformer lugs. Connect the ground wire in the power outlet cable to the ground wire in the transformer. Alternatively, you can use a plug-in transformer. Ensure that the plug-in outlet for the transformer is GFCI protected.

Lay your conduit from the transformer to the last lamp post while ensuring you have attached vertical facing tee couplers appropriately in the sections that will join to the lamp posts. Connect the transformers line wires to the corresponding hot wires in the conduit. Connect the neutral and ground wires of the transformer to the corresponding wires in the conduit.

Using snap-on connectors, attach the lamp post wires to the wires in the main run conduit via the vertical facing tee coupler. This is a simple process that does not require you to completely strip the wires in the main run conduit. Sharp edges of the snap-on connectors are able to pierce through the wire insulations and come in contact with the conductors. Use glue and seal all the jointed areas of the conduit to secure all the wires inside. Turn on the power to test if all the lamps are working. Use a voltmeter to measure the stability of the flow of low-voltage current in the wires.

Once your wiring has been inspected and approved by your building inspector, cover the trench with loose soil to conceal the conduit. At this point, you will effectively have completed the installation of your low-voltage outdoor lighting.

Motion Sensing Outdoor Lighting
A motion sensor outdoor light turns on with the slightest detection of movement. It is a security feature that you can install in sensitive areas of your home compound, such as unguarded entrances, to detect and expose trespassers at night. Except for its unique features and functional capabilities, the wiring and installation

process of motion sensor lighting is similar to procedures applied in other types of outdoor lighting. However, motion sensor lighting is not limited to the home landscape or garden. There are many other applications where this type of lighting is used as a smart home application.

Underwater Lighting for Swimming Pool and Spa

In most cases, wiring for swimming pool and spa lighting is done during construction. But you can still install a wiring circuit in an existing pool, as long as you drain the water and seek relevant approval from your local authority. All the materials used in swimming pool wiring are waterproof because they are specifically designed for that purpose.

If you have a connection to a swimming pool pump already, you can use a junction box to tap power from its wires. This will help you save time and reduce the distance of your wiring running all the way to the house or any other power source location. Disconnect power at the sub-panel for the swimming pool pump before you begin work.

Drill holes on the pool walls for fitting the electrical boxes that will house the lighting fixtures. Identify the shortest, but safe, distance between the outer wall of the swimming pool and the buried conduit for the swimming pool pump. Dig a trench to connect the two points. Use a chisel and hammer or a drill to penetrate the concrete around the swimming pool. Use the same tools to dig a channel along the swimming pool wall, all the way to the holes of electrical boxes. Mount the electrical boxes in place and screw them firmly in position

Cut out a small section of the swimming pool pump conduit to expose the cables. Cut the wires and strip the insulation at the tips. Install a junction box and use connectors to attach the wires. Strip the insulation from the tip points of the wires on the conduit you want to connect to the pool. Insert the hot, neutral, and ground wires to the respective connectors to tap power from the conduit run for the swimming pool pump.

Run the conduit all the way to the last electrical box. Use tee PVC pipes or elbow joints to change conduit direction or to direct a conduit to an electrical box. Use fish tape to pull wires into the electrical boxes. Connect the line and neutral wires into the lighting outlets, mount the outlets onto the electrical boxes, and screw them tight. Make sure that all joints along the conduit are sealed tightly with glue to avoid leakages. Cover the trench on the ground and the conduit channel on the pool wall. Fix bulbs of your choice and turn on the power to test if they are working properly.

Remember that in the current state, the swimming pool lighting will operate concurrently with the swimming pool pump because you have tapped its electrical power from the latter. Therefore, you need to install a separate switch for the lighting if you want it to operate independently of the swimming pool pump. Alternatively, rather than tap your electricity from underground conduits of other equipment, you can connect your swimming pool lighting system directly to the power source in the house via a sub-panel. You do not need to connect your swimming pool lighting to a GFCI-protected receptacle.

Chapter Summary

- The design and layout of your outdoor wiring must take into account the receptacle, lighting, and cabling codes for outdoor electrical installations.
- Outdoor electrical installations should always have grounding wire for protection against risks, such as lightning strikes.
- The installation process of the low-voltage outdoor wiring begins with the mapping out of the layout of the wiring runs.

In the next chapter, you will learn the basic components of home automation and networking.

Chapter Five: Home Automation and Networking

Home automation is a concept that has been around for many years. However, it was previously an expensive affair that was reserved for the wealthy. The tide has since turned following the advent of innovative networking protocols, such as the IoT, and other technological advancements that have reduced the cost of ownership. Home networking, on the other hand, creates interconnections among devices and between the devices and the internet. This is achieved through both wireless and wired networks.

Home Automation

Home automation is simply the delegation of the performance of tasks to artificially intelligent devices and appliances in your home. It is a robotic-like experience where devices use artificial intelligence capabilities to get a variety of things done, including switching lights on and off, controlling temperature, locking and unlocking the house, and monitoring the home environment, among other tasks. Smart home devices are mainly controlled using smartphones or smart assistants, such as Apple's Siri and Amazon's Alexa.

Home automation is a branch of the larger IoT domain. Internet-connected electrical devices that use artificial intelligence capabilities to detect and process instructions, otherwise known as connected devices, are crucial components of the home automation ecosystem, as well.

Home automation has transformed the nature and scope of electrical wiring and networking in modern homes. That is because home automation involves the installation of a central system for establishing connectivity among different electrical devices in your home, and facilitating the remote manipulation of the functions of those devices. As such, the widespread use of connected devices has necessitated the accommodation of home automation concepts in the overall electrical wiring design.

Fundamental Structural Components of a Smart Home

The transformation of your home into a smart home involves installing and connecting IoT devices and networks. The IoT is equipped with sensors alongside intelligent systems to provide the infrastructure for networking devices and supporting communication among the different devices. This makes it possible for the devices to perform designated tasks without user input. Some of the common installations that are associated with smart home transformation include door locks, lighting, audio systems, and surveillance cameras. Smart home operations are anchored on terminal devices, controllers, wireless network protocols, and internet connection.

Wireless Protocols

Wi-Fi is the most readily available network protocol for devices. Turning on the device Wi-Fi feature and a password is all that is needed to establish a Wi-Fi connection. But Wi-Fi has its own limitations that sometimes cripple the operations of smart home devices. For example, Wi-Fi disconnection due to sudden internet unavailability stalls the automated functionalities of all the smart home devices connected to it.

There are alternative wireless protocols, including ZigBee, Z-Wave, and Thread. You could alternatively deploy Bluetooth wireless protocol, as well. These proprietary wireless protocols are designed to help you overcome some of the challenges of using the Wi-Fi in your smart home. Unlike Wi-Fi, these wireless protocols do not require internet connectivity to operate. You can use ZigBee or Z-Wave in combination with Wi-Fi via a hub connection. The Google-owned Thread wireless protocol is a bit different because it is not compatible with Wi-Fi.

ZigBee and Z-Wave are actually classified as low power protocols with short-range wireless networking capabilities. They specifically use unique mesh technology to spread their network to all parts of your home. Mesh technology contains functional properties that allow signals to bounce from one device to the next in a zig-zag or wave-like pattern. This way, ZigBee and Z-Wave wireless protocols are able to spread network coverage to every part of your home that has a compatible device installed.

Hub

The hub, also known as a central controller, is an app-accessible component for establishing automated coordination among different smart home devices. It is actually the gateway point for conveying and processing communication between the different devices. This means that the hub is equipped with artificial intelligence capabilities for filtering and conveying signals and instructions across devices. For example, if you want the lights to shut off automatically whenever you step out of a room or the house, the controller is responsible for coordinating the sensors and lighting devices to respond accordingly.

The hub is useful in managing individual devices within the smart home network. Its user interface actually lets you use a smartphone app or web browser application to define the operational scopes of individual devices. Zigbee and Z-Wave transmit data via the hub, which actually helps in the conversion of sensor-conveyed data to the MQ Telemetry Transport (MQTT) format.

Terminal Devices

Switches, lighting installations, and sensors are some of the common terminal devices you will be interacting with when installing the different components of your smart house. Devices that are compatible with home network protocols, such as Wi-Fi or TCP, are easy to deploy in the IoT environment. This is because you only need to use a smartphone to establish direct connectivity between such devices and these common types of network protocols. For other devices that are anchored on either the ZigBee or the Z-Wave protocols, it will require the intervention of a hub to connect them to the internet.

Control Protocols

Smart home operations expose you to interactions with a variety of control protocols. Although the Hypertext Transmission Protocol (HTTP) is more or less the standard protocol for accessing websites, MQTT is actually the preferable control protocol for use in the IoT environment. HTTP is mostly used in cases where the compatibility of a device is not tied to any particular language protocol.

Security

Keeping your smart home secure from possible hacking attacks is one of the major concerns you will ordinarily have when installing your wiring system. Although hackers are always lurking all over the place and could compromise your smart home installations with the slightest opportunity, it should not be a source of major concern. There are various solutions that you can deploy to protect your smart home, including the use of strong passwords and frequent change of passwords. It is also important to encrypt your Wi-Fi connection to secure it from potential hacking.

Home Networking

The basic structure of home networking consists of network cables, ethernet, and Wi-Fi connections. Networking components support connectivity for a variety of devices, including computers, TVs, audio systems, printers, and other home appliances. Home networks are powered mainly by TCP and IP internet protocols. There are several other wireless protocol alternatives highlighted earlier in this chapter.

Some of the widely used terms used to describe home networks include a Local Area Network (LAN), Wide Area Network (WAN), and Wireless Fidelity (Wi-Fi) network. LAN involves creating connections between two or more devices using network cables. Apart from connecting devices to a shared connection point, usually a router, the network cables also connect the devices to shared peripheral devices, such as printers. LAN is mainly used in networking computers by attaching a computer's LAN port to the router's LAN port. You will also encounter names such as the RJ45 connectors and ethernet port, which are used in reference to the termination points of networked wires and cables. Creating a wired network simply involves plugging an ethernet-ported device into a router. WAN is needed when you want to connect your devices to the internet.

The WAN port comes as an installed feature in the router. It is labeled by a different color and installed some distance from the LAN ports. To establish a wired internet connection, simply connect an ethernet-ported device into the WAN port on the router. Network cables are more preferred for internet connections because they provide faster data processing speed. CAT5 and CAT6 are the widely used cable varieties in home networking.

A wireless network has arguably become the most widely used networking option because of the growth in the use of mobile devices. A wireless network is particularly suited for the smart home because of the multiplicity of devices that are used. Wi-Fi, for example, eliminates the tasks associated with setting up a cabled home network. Home networking is flexible to both wired and wireless networks and both can be used at the same time.

Wiring Closet

Rather than have the different components of your smart home scattered all over the place, you should install a wiring closet to house these items in one place. You may find a wiring closet useful in centralizing the location of the hardware components of your system. It allows you to have installations, such as the router, the ethernet switch, the patch panel, the telephone distribution block, and the video recorder, all in one place. This makes it easier for you to organize the distribution of wires and cables to different parts and installations in the house. The variety of hardware components in a wiring closet depends on the scope of your smart home automation. The closet contains racks and enclosed compartments to help you organize and tidy up your smart home network.

Structured Wiring Installation

The wired home network operates on the same principles as an office network, except for differences like the scope of the network and the output capacities of its installations. If you think about it in terms of structured wiring, you will identify significant differences in the composition of networked devices in a home compared to an office. Structured wiring touches on every single aspect of the communication, entertainment, automation, and security installations of your home network. Structured wiring actually consolidates the cabled connections across different devices and equipment within your home networking ecosystem. This consolidation helps create and distribute strong signals to all the networked devices and equipment.

Mount the wiring or distribution panel at the appropriate and readily accessible location to both data inlet and data outlet cables. If you have mounted a wiring closet already, this should be the priority location for your panel. You may also install the panel in the basement. If you are working on a tight budget, you can still do without the wiring panel and mount your cables and other wiring components on the wall, where you will terminate them with RJ45 connectors. However, this will present a lot of complications in the future when you need to diagnose and fix problems. Lack of a central termination point for your cables will make it cumbersome to test and identify faulty cables, jacks, or connectors.

Crosscheck to ensure that there are corresponding terminals for all the incoming cables in the wiring panel. This includes the internet switch, phone splitter, DSL modem, TV splitter, and router, among others. For example, cabling for the internet will use the DSL modem inlet terminal and the internet switch outlet.

Run the incoming cables of all the utility services, such as telephone, internet, and TV, to the wiring panel. Estimate the length that you will need for the incoming cable to reach their respective terminal points. As usual, leave some slack on the cables for flexible manipulation during their installation to the box. Cut the wires at the appropriate lengths and use connectors to attach each of the incoming data wires to the respective input terminals.

Shift your focus to output data wires and termination point connections. You may choose to start with the telephone, where you will use connectors to match the different strands wires of the phone to their respective ports in a patch panel located within the wiring panel. Alternatively, a phone splitter with multiple ports could simplify the process for you because it only requires the insertion of split wires from one end to the other through the holes in a connector. You will then use a crimping tool to attach the wires to the connector. Remember to tidy up the connector by trimming the inserted wires hanging from the backside.

In the event that you will be directing your phone line via the DSL modem, filter the phone signals within the DSL cable. You can do this using filters that you insert in phone jacks. The phone splitter installed in your wiring panel will be sufficient as per the conventions of structured wiring. The signal filters that you have established in the DSL cable will allow the splitter to concurrently have both a DSL output line and a patch panel-linked telephone line. This eliminates the need for separate splitters connecting to different phones within the house.

Proceed to the internet connectivity bit by inserting the cable modem to the DSL port in the wiring panel. Use CAT5 or CAT6 cable to establish a connection with the internet switch for distribution to the designated consumption points. Install a network switch as well, to be able to implement multiple internet connections. The network switch provides a jack for connecting the output cable of the DSL modem to provide multiple channels for connecting cabled internet to different sections of the house.

Ensure that all the coaxial cables and their corresponding cable TV connections are up to standard. The coaxial cable actually requires crimping in the connector prior to its attachment to the splitter. Strip the tip of the coaxial wire, slide the braid part of the wire backward, and insert the coaxial wire to the connector and crimp it right away. There should be no contact between the braid wire and the core. And if you are connecting inlet and outlet cables for a satellite, you will need to split the cable using a satellite multiplexer. Remember that all the inlet cables coming from the outside to the wiring panel must be grounded. The grounding feature is provided in most splitters.

Wi-Fi Installation

Wi-Fi installation basically needs a wireless router and an Access Point. If you have a LAN/WAN router connected in your home already, you are good to go, because you can still use it as a wireless router. Just buy a Wi-Fi Access Point and connect it to the router to add the Wi-Fi to the wired network in your house. If you do not have a router in place, you need to buy one, along with the Access Point.

Load the required data bundles of your service provider to test if the Wi-Fi is functioning. You can test the Wi-Fi on your smartphone or any other Wi-Fi ready device. Check for the Wi-Fi signal and load websites to test the strength of the signal. Also, test the strength of the signal in different parts of your house and compound. Your Wi-Fi bandwidth should stretch a recommended distance of 150 feet from the location of the Access Point. But remember that the strength of the Wi-Fi will not be the same in all devices. The signal tends to be strong in more sophisticated devices that are sufficiently equipped with advanced Wi-Fi features compared to the low-end devices.

If everything works well, you will have accomplished your Wi-Fi installation mission. But if you encounter problems, such as weak signals, keep moving the location of the access point until you locate the desired signal quality. If that doesn't work as well, contact your network service provider for help. You could also try to find out if the Wi-Fi Access point has a manufacturing default. Exercise your warranty and exchange it for a proper one if you detect a manufacturer default.

Important Wi-Fi Connection Tips

Once you have installed your Wi-Fi, the speed will vary with your data plan but also with other functionality and operational factors. For example, the Wi-Fi standard specification has a bearing on the maximum coverage distance of the Wi-Fi installation. The other complication presented by the Wi-Fi standard is that it dictates the data speed of your Wi-Fi, regardless of the bandwidth in use, and there is not much that you can do about it, because the situation is fueled by factors that are beyond your control.

Annual releases of Wi-Fi standards date back to 1999 when 802.11b was unveiled, and there have been many releases since then. The latest Wi-Fi release will always come with advanced compatibility features designed to accommodate advancements in telecommunication technologies. Ensure that the Wi-Fi Access Point is configured to work with the current network in your area. For example, do not buy an Access Point with 5G network configurations when your service provider is yet to upgrade from a 4G network.

The other important tip to consider concerns the frequency band. The Wi-Fi standard again comes into play here because it is functionally intertwined with the radio frequency bands. You are most likely to interact with either the 2.4GHz or the 5.0GHz band because they are the two common band options available for Wi-Fi connections.

Power Line Carrier
A power line carrier provides a convenient alternative for converting your electrical wiring into a multipurpose system by using it as a networking platform, as well. This is done through the use of special adapters. Power line

adapters are actually installed to the router and the second one is installed on the destination point of an ethernet-ready device.

Some of the use cases of a power line carrier include extending the coverage of your wired or Wi-Fi networks to outdoor locations. For example, rather than laying new network cabling in your newly constructed outbuilding, you could instead opt to exploit the electrical wiring in the outbuilding to achieve internet connectivity. This method is also useful in low-lying areas or areas separated by unusually thick concrete that are impenetrable to Wi-Fi, such as basements. You could also find a power line carrier solution helpful when in need of a quick but cost-saving fix to supply an internet connection to a location such as a garage.

The X10 Automation Technology

X10 automation technology for the smart home is almost similar to the power line carrier because it uses existing electrical wiring connections to support automated communication among devices. The system uses radio frequencies to provide remote-controlled operation lighting, security, appliances, and outdoor installations in your home. The use of x10 transmitters and receivers facilitates the conveyance of module commands through the existing wiring system. You simply need a remote control to turn switches on and off. X10 home automation technology is compatible with a variety of wireless devices. It can also be used in combination with wireless protocols, such as ZigBee and Z-Wave.

The x10 infrastructure in your house will primarily consist of a transmitter and a receiver. The transmitter is the device that bears the control signals. You can either plug in the device or establish a direct connection for the device in your wiring system. The transmitter signal travels through your electrical wiring system to deliver instruction to switches and controllers. For example, a switch-on light signal should automatically prompt the lights to turn on upon receipt of the command by a receiver. The receiver is also plugged in or wired into the system's outlets to act on transmitted commands. Wireless signals are instrumental in the broadcasting of wireless signals between the transmitters and transceivers. The transceiver is a wireless component that helps transform radio frequency signals into x10 instructions that are implemented by the receiver.

Chapter Summary

- Artificial intelligence and IoT are the primary drivers of home automation applications and devices.
- Wireless protocols, such as ZigBee and Z-Wave, do not require internet connectivity to power automated home devices and appliances.
- There are various solutions for protecting the automated home from potential attacks by hackers.

In the next chapter, you will learn about the basic structure and logistical parameters of electricity.

Chapter Six: Functional and Logistical Parameters of Electricity

Electricity is the energy that flows through wired connections to power devices, appliances, and equipment at home, in organizations, or in industries. It is a broad term that describes a chain of reactions that occur within the structure of an atom to generate charge from the movement of electrons relative to the statuses of protons and neutrons. To better understand the dimension of each of these components in electricity creation, let's briefly explore the structure of an atom.

The atom – that is, the smallest unit of matter, has a nucleus at its center which in turn hosts protons and neutrons. Whereas protons are the positively charged particles, neutrons bear no charge. The nucleus is surrounded by electrons that operate as negatively charged particles. The number of protons inside the nucleus is equal to the number of electrons outside the nucleus. A shift in this balance sets the electrons in motion in a process that results in the creation of electric power. This is because the electron serves as the primary charge carrier and its movement from the atom creates electricity and electric field.

Generation, Distribution, and Utilization

The infrastructure of electricity supply begins right from the point of generation and this could be hydroelectric power, geothermal power, solar power, or wind turbines. Electricity is also generated from coal, biomass and industrial waste, nuclear power, and gas-powered generators. These power sources are configured to facilitate the conversion of either mechanical energy or chemical energy to electrical power.

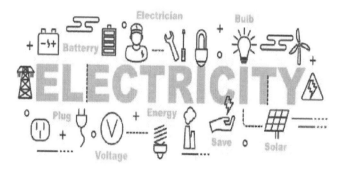

The energy conversion process takes place with the help of the electric generator, which provides the mechanisms required to induce electricity-generating interactions between a magnetic field and an electric conductor. This conductor exists as a fixed installation inside an electric generator that also contains a mobile magnetized shaft. The shaft is fitted right inside a fixed ring-shaped conductor and is covered by a stretch of electric wire. The rotation of the magnetized shaft automatically brings small currents of electric current to life along the different sections of the stretching wire. These small currents gradually accumulate into a larger current size that finally exits as electricity from the electrical generator. The generated electricity is transported through a high-voltage grid to transmission substations before it is distributed for consumption through a network of transformers.

The measurement of the units of electric power is expressed in watts. But the watt, being the smallest unit of measurement for electricity consumption, requires a lot of digits to capture the actual consumption details. It is for this reason that the watt is converted to the kilowatt at a ratio of 1000 to 1. That is why your electric meter reading is expressed in terms of a kilowatt-hour (kWh) – that is, the number of kilowatts you have consumed multiplied by the number of hours of your electricity use.

Current Flow versus Current Resistance

Current flow is the smooth transmission and distribution of electricity between different points. There must be current flow all the time for your plugged appliances and lighting fixtures to operate. But the power flow is disrupted when you shut down your panels, breakers, or switches. Power flow can also be interrupted by damaged components within your wiring system.

Current resistance, on the other hand, is a force that derails the flow of power between two points. As such, current resistance does not entirely shut down power flow. Rather, the power will keep flowing, albeit at below optimum levels. The level of resistance determines the flow of charge in a conduit. The higher the resistance, the less the power flow, and vice versa. The value of resistance is often expressed using the omega – that is, the Ω, sign of Greek letters.

The ohm law best explains resistance and how it occurs in an electrical system. According to ohm law, the resistance of an ohm unit is the equivalent of the prevailing resistance along the stretch connecting two points in an electric wire, whereby the injection of a particular voltage will push a corresponding number of amperes. This means that the voltage in a particular conduit is a direct consequence of the combination of current and resistance. To this end, ohm expresses this form of resistance using the formula below.

$V = A.R$

Whereby V, A, and R will be the voltage, current, and resistance, respectively.

Therefore, if a conductor with 5-ohm resistance between two points is exposed to 5 volts, it will push a corresponding 5 amps of current. There, the calculation for resistance is as shown below.

$$5V = 5A.1 \ \Omega$$

Safety Considerations

When working with electricity, it only takes a split of a second for disaster to strike. Therefore, safety must always be a paramount consideration in your home wiring operations. Other than wearing safety gear, there are many other procedural precautions that you must always take before, during, and after wiring. Always shut down power in the main panel or sub-panels, depending on the section you are working on, if you are renovating an existing wiring system. You must also shut down power if tapping power for your outdoor wiring from an indoor outlet. Never attempt to test for electric current with your bare hands because that is the easiest way to get electrocuted. Always use a tester to check for the flow of electric current in wires and cables.

In the event that the wiring transitions from a four-conductor cable to a three-conductor cable, or vice versa, you can still proceed to establish a connection between the cables. The easiest bit is connecting the ground wires because they are an obvious match. However, you should be careful to not connect the ground wire of either of the cable to the neutral of the other. This would be disastrous because such an error of commission overhauls the operational dynamics of the circuit. It is a faulty connection that actually transforms the neutral wire into a live status because it closes the circuit the moment you insert a plug into the outlet. The ground conductor also goes live by virtue of its connection to the neutral.

Similarly, do not leave the ground wire hanging hazardously because of the belief that it serves no significant purpose in the wiring system. Contrary to this perception, you must connect the ground wire at all times. The purpose of the ground wire is to interrupt sudden surge in the flow of electric current and trip the circuit breaker. This neutralizes the danger or damage that the surge in electric current will have caused. When you leave the ground wire unconnected, the circuit breaker will not trip and poses risk, such as shocks and fire, as well as damage to the wiring system and appliances.

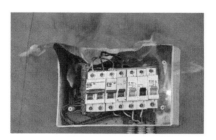

It gets a bit tricky to connect live wires and decide which of the live wires in the four-conductor cable to connect to the live wire of the three-conductor cable. The best approach is to pair the black wire in the three-conductor cable with either the red or black wire in the four-conductor cable. The beautiful thing about electrical wiring is that you can use either of the live wires in the four-conductor cable to power your circuits.

Key Electrical Terminologies

This book has used various terminologies to describe different components and aspects of electrical wiring and electricity as a whole. This section provides a summary of the major terms that will help you to better understand the different topics. This is not an exhaustive list of all the electrical terms, but rather a selection of the relevant terms that have been used in this book. Electricity is a broad topic and you will keep encountering more terms as you broaden your knowledge about this particular subject matter.

Charge is one of the properties of matter. Charge can be positive or negative and is measurable like any other property of matter, such as mass and density. The flow of charge is basically what defines the flow of electricity.

Conductivity is the ability of conductors to carry electric power between different points within a wiring system. These conductors bear certain levels of conductivity to be able to convey electric signals between different points. Therefore, conductivity is the degree to which electrons are attached to atoms. The more tightly the electrons are attached to an atom, the less suitable a conductor is for electric power transmission and vice versa.

Electric current describes the rate of the flow of electric charge and mainly refers to the motion aspect of electricity. The term is quite common in wiring operations because of the nature of current contained in the different wires of a cable. For example, the hot, neutral, and ground wires in an electric cable carry active current, while the ground cable carries zero current.

Electric fields occur when charges push and pull against each other to create a force between them. It is instrumental in determining the flow of electricity between different points.

Electrostatic force defines the attraction or repellant relationship between positive and negative charges. It operates like magnetism whereby positive charges are only attracted to negative charges, or vice versa. Charges with similar orientations repel each other. This push and pull actions among different charges is the mechanism that occurs between electrons and neutrons to create electricity. Electrostatic is also known as Coulomb's Law.

Resistance is the disruption of the smooth flow of current between two points in a circuit. Resistance is imposed by external force, such as material resistance, on the path of the current flow. As already demonstrated in this chapter, resistance is closely associated with current and voltage in the ohm law calculations of electricity flow. However, resistance should not be confused with static electricity - the two terms refer to the prevalence of completely different situations in the electric circuit.

Static electricity prevails when insulator-protected objects accumulate opposite charges, a kind of stalemate will ensue. This stalemate is known as static electricity because the charges on both ends are immobilized until such a time when a path is created across the insulator to restore the flow of charges. Static electricity is the opposite of electrical current.

Voltage is a commonly used term to describe the flow of charge between two points and the actual difference of the output of charge between the two points. Voltage is widely used to indicate the capacity output for receptacles and outlets, with 120 volts and 240 volts being the common ones.

Chapter Summary

- The electric generator provides the mechanisms required to induce electricity-generating interactions between a magnetic field and an electric conductor.
- The flow of electricity along a conductor is dictated by the movement of the electrons.
- Electric current resistance is a force that interrupts the smooth flow of power to receptacles and outlets.

In the next chapter, you will learn the common mistakes electricians make and how to avoid them.

Chapter Seven: Seven Mistakes Most Electricians Make and How to Avoid Them

Electrical wiring is always a delicate process from the start to the end of any given DIY project at home. You should never become overconfident when dealing with electricity. It is common to unknowingly commit some mistakes and some of them could be fatal. Some mistakes expose you and other users to electrocution, some damage your appliances, while others cause fire. For example, U.S. Fire Administration Statistics cited in Sirikit Hiyasmin Eleberan's May 2, 2018 blog on the US Electrical Services Inc. website revealed that about 6.3 percent, or about 24,000 of residential fires, were attributable to electrical fires. This underscores the significance of keeping tabs on all the crucial areas that are prone to electrical wiring mistakes. Below is a summary of the seven common mistakes that electricians commit and how to avoid them.

Undermining the Significance of Junction Boxes

The number one common mistake that electricians make is to avoid the installation of junction boxes at the contact points of wire connections. On many occasions, an electrician will simply wrap electrical tape around the wire joints or leave the joints exposed. The exposed wire joint connections can accidentally be pulled apart by physical force, while tape insulations can loosen over time and gradually expose naked joints. This is ultimately a recipe for disaster, especially if the line, neutral, and ground wire connections come into contact.

To avoid this mistake, install joint boxes appropriately in sections where you have multiple joints for wire connections. A joint box will secure all the wire connections firmly in position and secure the joints from the impact of high-voltage currents that occasioned by incidences such as power surges and short circuits.

Congestion of Wires in Electrical Boxes

The number two common mistake committed by electricians in wiring projects involves inserting way too many wires in a single electrical box. Such stuffing of wires occurs when an electrician creates many cable lines required to supply power to a large variety of devices and appliances in the house. Overstuffing electrical boxes can potentially cause short circuit because of the high likelihood of wires coming into contact with at the terminal points of outlets.

You can avoid this mistake by purchasing a larger electrical box that will accommodate all your wires. Also refer to the NEC requirements for electrical box installation to determine the permissible number of the hot, neutral, and ground wires for a particular box size. Electrical box size calculation is the other viable solution for this mistake. The procedure for calculating the appropriate box size for your wires is discussed in great detail already in chapter three of this book.

Leaving Cables Exposed

It is common practice to leave plastic insulated electric cables in locations such as framing members. Having hazardous hanging cables in your ceiling framing and behind your walls is not the best approach to wiring. It will present challenges whenever you need to cut holes in your walls during repairs or installation of new cables. You will face the risk of damaging or cutting through cables during such operations. This particular mistake also amounts to blatant contravention of the NEC requirement that all cables located between framing members must be insulated. Therefore, this mistake will earn you a direct disqualification from your building inspector.

The recommended solution for this mistake is to conceal cables behind a nailed board with considerable thickness to provide protection. You may consider using a 1.5-inch thick board to cover the cables. The use of a conduit will be another appropriate alternative, especially for the vertical and horizontal wire runs along the wall.

Providing Insufficient Lengths for Wire Connections

The number four mistake you are likely to commit as an electrician is using short cables for your connections. This mostly happens when you underestimate the total length of cables and wires that you will need for your project. It may also happen accidentally when you underestimate the cable length you will require to establish a connection between two points. Overstretching the conductors in your wire could increase current resistance in your wiring system. Your wires could also snap and detach from the terminals and disrupt the flow of electrical power to particular outlets.

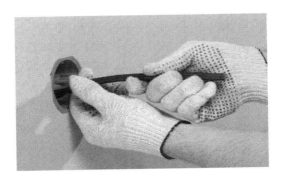

The recommended solution for this mistake is to provide sufficient slack in your measurements so that your cable can fit properly between different points. You also need to provide extensions of at least 6 inches for wires in electric boxes to be able to fit your receptacles and other outlets conveniently.

Incorrect Alignment of Electrical Boxes on the Walls

The process of attaching electric boxes on studs requires precision and accuracy because the box must eventually lie flush to the drywall. However, it is common for an electrician to ignore this requirement and install an electrical box too deep, so it remains in a sunken position once the drywall is installed. This is dangerous because drywall is made of flammable material that could easily catch fire, should the wires in the electrical box ignite sparks.

The installation of a box extension is the recommended solution for fixing a sunken electrical box and bringing it to flush position with the drywall. The box extension saves you the time and energy you otherwise will spend on removing and reinstalling the box. You will most probably select a plastic box extension for your plastic electrical box. But you may select a metallic box extension, as long as you remember to attach a grounding wire connection to the extension.

Loosely Attached Outlets and Switches

Mistake number six you are likely to commit as an electrician is a failure to tighten outlets and switches in your wiring system. This could happen when the screws attaching the outlets are not connected to firm support behind the drywall. The screws may not be holding tight because of wide holes or errors during the initial installation. A loosely attached outlet or switch could easily flip over or even fall off the wall and expose every single person in your house to the risk of electric shock. If loose wires in such outlets become prone to arcing, the risk of fire will prevail, as well.

Fixing loose outlets may require simple remedies, such as filling up the screw holes and screwing the outlet tightly again. Small instruments, such as washers, could also help you correct this anomaly. If nothing else works, consider removing the faulty outlet or switch and installing it in a different location. The last solution might be a demanding task, but always remember that safety must always come first in all the electrical installation in your house.

Running Cables without Clamps

Failure to use clamps when installing cables is the other common mistake that electricians commit. This is not an issue with plastic boxes because they are fitted with built-in catches for holding cables firmly in place. However, if you have installed metallic boxes, you need to use cable clamps to hold your cables in position.

In the event that you come across a metal box in which the cables have not been secured appropriately using clamps, simply install the clamps to fix the problem. Strap the cables under the clamps once you are done fixing the clamps.

Chapter Summary

- The junction box plays a crucial role in keeping jointed areas of wire connections safe.
- Concealing cables located between framing members helps secure electrical wires from potential damage.
- Loose outlets and receptacles must be attended to with urgency because they pose fire and electrocution risks.

In the next chapter, you will learn to install and connect solar electric power to your home wiring system.

Chapter Eight: Solar Electric System Installation and Wiring

Solar electric system, also known as photovoltaic (PV) system, is a renewable energy source that is used to substitute or supplement the electric power that we use every other day. Energy is generated using solar modules that absorb and convert sunlight into operating voltage. The energy is suited for use in your home or for supply to the utility transmission grid.

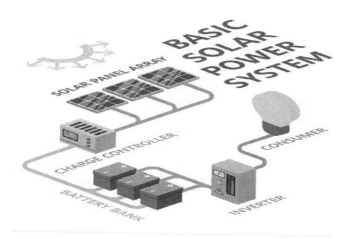

Solar electric power generation varies with seasonal patterns because this type of energy is solely dependent on sunlight. Energy output will ordinarily be high during summer and hit the lowest levels during the winter months. However, other factors, such as your geographic location and the specific weather and climatic conditions in that particular location, will dictate the power generation dynamics of your PV system.

Types of Solar Electric Systems

Grid-connected and non-grid connected PV systems are the most widely installed types of solar power in residential buildings. A grid-connected system makes you both a supplier and consumer of electricity. You will use an inverter to transform the power generated by the PV system from direct current (DC) to alternating current (AC). The power is transmitted through an inverter AC disconnect installation, where it branches to a main electrical panel for connection to the grid and a sub-panel for solar energy loads from the power backup source.

A utility electric meter connected between the main service panel and your power provider's utility transmission grid records the wattage of your power supply. In the meantime, you can continue to consume your electricity from the same grid and the utility electrical meter will capture the trends of your consumption, as well. This process is known as net energy metering because it provides you the opportunity to earn credits for the extra power that you contribute to the grid. You will ideally be storing energy to the grid in the daytime, when solar power generation is at its optimum, and consuming the power at night, when your solar electric system is no longer generating power.

The grid-connected system is further classified into grid-connected AC with battery backup and grid-connected AC without battery backup. The former provides backup to connected installations when there is an interruption of power supply from your utility provider's transmission line. But if you are seeking a system that generates more power for distribution to the grid, you will have to select the one without battery backup because it is capable of generating between 200 volts and 600 volts. This is quite high compared to the battery-backed PV system that generates power output ranging between 12 volts and 48 volts.

Installation of a non-grid connected system simply means that you will be consuming all your PV system-generated power. In this system, you will connect your AC-converted power to the main service panel for distribution to outlets within your house. Such a system can also be installed to operate specific indoor or outdoor equipment and appliances. For example, you can install a PV system for specific use in powering your water heaters or swimming pool pumps.

Materials and Equipment

The installation procedure of a PV wiring system is not fundamentally different from that of grid-supplied electric power supplied through your provider's utility transmission system. However, some of the materials and equipment you require are quite different from the ones used in routine electrical wiring. You also need to pay special attention to the wiring and conduit materials, as well as the other outdoor installations that you deploy in your system. It is recommended to use weatherproof materials for safety and durability of your solar electric system.

The specifications and scope of the materials actually depend on your type of PV system installation. For example, in addition to all the materials that you require for a grid-connected installation without battery backup, you will require extras, like battery banks and charge controllers for a grid-connected installation with battery backup. Materials required for a grid-connected residential system without battery backup include solar modules, mounting racks, grounding equipment, combine box (or junction box), inverter, and disconnects.

The solar module is the primary source of energy for electric power generation. It contains built-in properties and semiconductor materials responsible for converting light, or photons, into energy. In fact, the semiconductor materials in the solar module operate in a similar fashion to the electric conductor during the creation of electricity. The electrons in the atoms within the semiconductor materials are activated by the exposure of the solar module to light. It is the force of motion in electrons that pushes them along the semiconductor and this generates electricity.

There are different types of solar modules, the common ones being crystalline and CdTe modules. Crystalline modules are further classified into single-crystalline and polycrystalline categories. The CdTe module consists of thin-film material that carries its energy generation properties. The durability, efficiencies, and output capacity of any given solar module depends on its material composition. For example, a crystalline module costs more that a CdTe module because crystalline silicon material is durable and contains more power generation and transmission capabilities compared to the thin-film material.

An array mounting rack is useful for installing your modules on the rooftop or any other appropriate location. Rooftop racks provide a gap for air circulation between roof surfaces and modules. They also help you secure your PV system modules firmly to avoid the risk of falling off and causing damage. Some array racks have adjustable features for turning the angles of the solar modules relative to the seasonal changes of the position of the sun, especially for modules that are installed in open space areas.

Grounding equipment is a safety precaution for protecting your solar electric system from potential power surges and other electrolytic risks. Solar power grounding equipment is functionally similar to those used in wiring installations for electricity supplied by your power utility provider. It is designed to diffuse excess current flows in your wiring system by safely diverting it to the ground. As such, it consists of both equipment and system grounding. Equipment grounding serves the purpose of protecting your electrical system from destabilization by shock incidences that are attributable to ground fault. System grounding in a solar electric system involves creating a connection between the negative wire and the ground to help divert excess current flows in a DC system.

A combiner box is more or less a junction box that serves as the destination point for wires running from each of your installed solar modules. These are typically the wires that are pre-installed as part of the solar module package. The combiner box consolidates the DC power input from the solar modules and channels it to the inverter via two conduit-protected wires. It also houses several safety features, including fuses and surge protectors.

A utility meter is the other important piece of equipment for your solar electric system. The utility meter measures the back and forth transmission of electric power in kWh between your solar electric system and the utility transmission line of your utility provider. This particular meter is customized to record current flow in either direction. You may also find the system meter useful in monitoring the overall performance of your solar electric system.

The primary motivation behind the inclusion of surge protectors is to secure your system from the impact of sudden fluctuations of current flow in the wiring system. There are also external risks, such as lighting, that could damage your system if not secured by a surge protector.

The inverter is a similarly crucial piece of equipment in solar power connections. As we have seen already earlier in this chapter, the inverter is useful in DC to AC power conversions. The inverter also helps stabilize the current flow and the voltage output of your system. There are different inverter types and sizes and your choice will depend on your target electricity generation output.

The disconnect is one of the unique safety features of a solar electric system and it plays the crucial role of interrupting the flow of current whenever the need arises. It is particularly useful for isolating power sources and storage components. For example, you need to install a disconnect device between the main electrical panel and the utility meter of a grid-connected system to establish a point of separation between your solar electric system and the utility transmission line. This particular disconnect is known as an exterior AC disconnect. The array DC disconnect, inverter DC disconnect, and inverter AC disconnect are the other types of disconnects present in an solar electric system.

Extras for Grid-Connected Battery Backup PV System

A grid-connected PV system with battery backup requires all the materials used for grid-connected system, plus charge controllers, a battery bank, and battery disconnects. The battery bank provides storage of the DC energy for a continuous power supply in the event of disruption of utility line-supplied power. Battery DC disconnect creates an isolation point for interrupting power flow between the battery and the rest of the system. Charge controllers, on the other hand, regulate the flow of current from the PV module to the battery. You need to protect your battery from sudden surges of current from the PV module as a result of the fluctuating patterns of light and temperature.

NEC Requirements for Solar Electric System

Just like the installation of an ordinary grid-powered electric system, the solar electric system is subject to the NEC guidelines. In fact, the NEC has a dedicated section for provisions that govern the PV system. These guidelines also touch on almost each and every component or device in your solar electrical system. For example, the NEC contains specific requirements for grounding, wiring sizes and installation, disconnect operations, and surge protection.

There are occasions where you will come across special NEC exemptions that are restricted to the PV system installation and operations. For example, NEC requirements do not caution against the use of single-cable conductors that are exposed when connecting a chain of solar modules. Such an exemption is not available for electric generator-sourced power supply. It is important to familiarize yourself with these guidelines before embarking on the actual installation of your system.

Solar Electric System Wiring Types

Solar electric system installation begins with the selection of an appropriate location. The rooftop is the most ideal and widely preferred installation location for solar modules. But this location must meet certain thresholds, such as the absence of shade from trees or other buildings. You have the choice of using either parallel or the series wiring when connecting your solar modules. You may also use a combination of both wiring options, depending on the structure and design of your PV system.

In a series wiring connection, the modules are chained together in a succession pattern. The first module in the queue is connected to the next one, which in turn is connected to the next one, in a pattern that is repeated until the last module is connected. The voltage of the entire string of modules is the sum of the voltage of the modules. However, the combined amperage of the entire string is the same as the amperage of a single module. This is because the current for all the modules in the string is transmitted along a single wire that cuts across the modules.

A parallel wiring connection involves channeling the module wire to the main wire running from the source. All the positive electrodes (red wires) are linked to a central red wire, while all the negative electrodes (black wires) are connected to a central black wire. It is like river tributaries joining the main river. When it comes to voltage and amperage counts, the parallel wiring is the exact opposite of the series wiring. The total amperage will be the sum of the amperage of all the modules in the connection. The voltage of the entire connection will be equal to the voltage of a single module in the connection because the modules are parallel to each other. Unlike series wiring, which has a single wire running from the source, parallel wiring has several wiring running from the power source.

Solar Module Efficiency

Efficiency in solar electric power generation concerns a solar module's potential to maximize the conversion of sunlight to electricity. An efficient solar module is one that minimizes the loss of energy by converting most of the energy that it absorbs into electricity. The Greek letter eta, usually denoted as η, is used to express the efficiency of a solar module.

Standard Testing Conditions (STC) and PVUSA Test Conditions (PTC) are some of the ratings that are used to determine eta in solar modules. STC ratings are laboratory-tested thresholds that manufacturers develop for use in determining the maximum output of a solar module with respect to the maximum number of watts, current, and voltage. STC also provides details concerning the voltage of the open circuit and current for short circuit connections. All these thresholds and details are always indicated on the specification descriptions of each solar module. This allows you to calculate the efficiency on the basis of the output of the different parameters.

The STC formula for module efficiency calculation is expressed as follows: (number of watts / (module area in m^2 x 1000w/m^2) x 100). Therefore, the efficiency for a 240W module measuring 1.8m^2 will be (240W / (1.8 m^2 x 1000w/m^2) x 100) = 13.3%.

The independently developed PTC rating is the alternative to the STC rating, especially if you are seeking to accurately determine the efficiencies associated with the output of a solar module. The use of PTC rating is a requirement in some states, including California. Its tests are based on real-world estimates of the environmental conditions that prevail in solar module installation locations. As such, conditions, like the intensity of the sunlight and the speed of the wind, are factored in the determination of the efficiency of a solar panel.

The PTC formula for module efficiency calculation is similar to that of STC. The difference lies in the size of ratings provided by the two methods because STC always provides a higher rating than PTC. In fact, lower PTC ratings are always considered to be reliable because they provide accurate ratings compared to PTC. For example, a 240W STC rating could actually be 220W in reality and that is why PTC uses the lower rating in calculations. Therefore, the efficiency for a 220W module measuring $1.8m^2$ will be (220W / (1.8 m^2 x 1000w/m^2) x 100) = 12.2%

PV System Circuit

The circuit layout of a solar electric wiring system is fundamentally similar to the other circuit types already discussed in this book. Your circuit must contain a conductor that connects the power source to the main electrical panel. The array is the primary source of power in a PV system. You also need to have a second line wire for channeling electrons back to the source to complete the circuit of electric power flow.

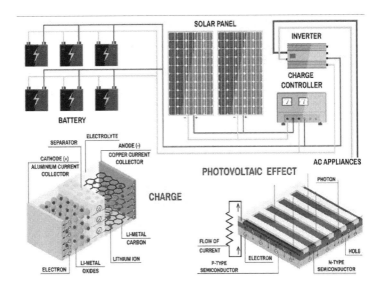

The ground wire is the third crucial component that you need to add to your wiring connections. Although the ground wire does not count as part of the solar electric wiring circuit, it still is an important safety requirement for connecting the hardware components of your electrical installations to the ground. This wire drives current to the ground in the event of a bare line wire coming into contact with a metal or any surface that is responsive to electric current. AWG 6 copper bare copper conductor is the recommended ground wire for use in your PV system because of its strength and weatherproof properties.

Balancing the Loads

The watt is the primary unit of measurement for solar electric energy. Multiply the module's voltage rating by the amperage of its electric current production to determine the watts. This underscores the significance of achieving a balance between the voltage and the amperage in the design and installation of your solar electric system. The best way to achieve the required load balance is to determine the combined wattage relative to the number of hours that your appliances will be in use.

For example, let's say you want to run a 60W radio, 120W television, 40W bulb, and 250W fridge for 5 hours, 3 hours, 4 hours, and 4 hours, respectively. The watt-hour for each of the components will be as follows:

Radio – 60W x 5H = 300
Television – 120W x 3H = 360
Bulb – 40W x 4H = 160
Fridge – 250W x 4H = 1000

This will give you a total watt-hour of 1,820 because the combined watt hour will be the sum of all components - you simply add the watt-hours of all these fixtures and appliances. You now need to factor in the average energy loss from your PV system. Let's assume the average power loss in your PV system is 20 percent. Multiply the total watt-hour by the percentage energy loss to get your

average load. This will be 1820 x 120/100 = 2,184.
However, take note that this example has used random
figures. You can always get the actual power rating of
your appliances in the specifications chart of each
appliance.

System Installation and Wiring Procedure

Gather your tools, materials, and equipment close to
the installation site. You also need a helping hand because
the installation of the solar module is quite a laborious
process. Lift the racks to the rooftop and screw them
firmly in position. Proceed to lift the solar modules to the
rooftop. Run the ground cable across all the modules and
connect it to the combiner box. Mount the modules to the
racks, using either the series or the parallel wiring pattern,
and screw them tightly, as well.

If you are working on a PV system without battery
backup, install all the required components, including the

combiner box, array disconnect, charge controller, system meter, inverter DC disconnect, inverter, inverter AC disconnect, and exterior AC disconnect. The main electrical panel and the utility meter should be in place already if your home is connected to grid electricity. The exterior AC disconnect installation should be located between the main electrical panel and the utility transmission meter.

If you are working on a PV system with battery backup, the structure will be similar to the one without battery backup with two major exceptions. You need to introduce a battery AC disconnect between the charge controller and the battery bank. You also have to install a sub-panel parallel to the main electrical panel for distributing solar electric power to outlets during a power outage.

Use connectors to attach the solar module wires to the combiner box. Attach the line and neutral wires in the exit conduit to the combiner box, as well. Run the conduit through the different components to establish interconnections between them and create a complete circuit. At this point, you will have completed your solar installation project.

Remember that this installation and wiring procedure is applicable to a house that already has an existing utility grid-powered electrical system in place. You have to start the rough-in wiring phase if you are installing your solar electric system in a house without any form of wiring and electricity supply.

Chapter Summary

- The installation of grid-connected solar provides an income-generating opportunity.
- Grid-connected AC solar power without battery backup is easier to install and maintain compared to grid-connected AC with battery backup.
- The efficiency of a solar module is determined by both its structural properties and the environmental conditions.

In the next chapter, you will learn to perform simple repairs and maintenance procedures for receptacles, switches, and other outlet installations in your wiring system.

Chapter Nine: Repairs and Maintenance Tips

Damaged outlets and plugs can easily compromise the efficiency of your wiring system, especially when upgrading an old system. Slight or major damage in any particular outlet could gradually transfer to other parts of the wiring system. Prioritize the repair or replacement of faulty switches and receptacles to avoid functional setbacks. Repair slightly damaged outlets and replace the ones with major damage.

Plug Replacement

The replacement of a damaged fuse may be sufficient to restore a malfunctioned plug head. But there are occasions when you may need to replace the entire plug head for the appliance to function properly. Connecting the red and the black wires to their respective terminals during repair or maintenance is a simple process. Screw the red to the plug's terminal and the black to its corresponding terminal. Since you will have attached the red and black wires to the brass terminals, this leaves you the silver and green terminals for the neutral and ground wires, respectively. The same process applies when swapping the heads of appliances, even when they are not necessarily damaged. Remember to test all the screws to ensure that they are tight and all the wires are in the right terminals before plugging your appliance.

Receptacle Replacement

You will always find the need to replace some damaged installations during a DIY renovation of an existing wiring system. Receptacles are no exception to such replacements because you must fix or replace all the physically damaged items. Some of the common damage associated with receptacles include cracking, widened plug holes that can no longer hold plugs in position, and aging due to wear and tear.

Ensure that you have switched off the circuit breaker that connects to the receptacle. Remove the top cover to expose the receptacle and its screws. Unscrew the receptacle from the electrical box. Pull out the receptacle from the electrical box and unscrew the line, neutral, and ground wire from the terminals of the old receptacle and remove it.

Take the new receptacle and loosen the terminal screws a bit for easy installation of the electrical box wires. Slide the line, neutral, and ground wires of the electrical box to the brass, silver, and green terminals of the receptacle, respectively. Screw the wires tight on the receptacles to hold them firm. Mount the replacement receptacle back into the electrical box and screw it tight into position. Attach the receptacle cover to complete the process. Turn on the circuit breaker and use a tester to verify if the installed receptacle is working.

Chapter Summary

- Repair of damaged receptacles and outlets helps you save costs associated with purchasing new replacements.
- Repair of damaged electrical outlets should be restricted to slightly damaged items.

Final Words

This book has covered the major topics of wiring, with particular emphasis on indoor and outdoor wiring, as well as home automation. The different tips that you have read in this book are designed to help you perform any given wiring task with reference to NEC requirements. It is always important to understand the relevance of the different requirements for your wiring tasks and projects.

The home automation topic has demonstrated the changing face of the home electrical system. Information technology has clearly become part and parcel of the electrical wiring ecosystem of the home. This is one area that will keep experiencing new innovations given the dynamic nature of information technology.

Image Credit: Shutterstock.com